Sessions:
All therapy supports relationships integrating toward unity

KEITH WITT, Ph.D.

Santa Barbara Graduate Institute Publishing

iUniverse, Inc.
New York   Bloomington

iUniverse books may be ordered through booksellers or by contacting:

iUniverse
1663 Liberty Drive
Bloomington, IN 47403
www.iuniverse.com
1-800-Authors (1-800-288-4677)

ISBN: 978-0-595-52926-1 (pbk)
ISBN: 978-0-595-62976-3 (ebk)

Printed in the United States of America

Contents

In the evening I saw you were fractured,
Pacing and raging, your mind on the line.
So I smiled and asked you,
Try just one more time.

~from *Fallen**~

*Unless otherwise indicated, all lyrics are from songs by Keith Witt and Larry Praisman

INTRODUCTION

Teilhard de Chardin, the famous Jesuit paleontologist, believed that evolution flows in the direction of increasing consciousness and greater unity[1]. This includes both the evolution of species and of each human from birth to death. Cosmologist Brian Swimme and historian Thomas Berry assert that evolution is characterized at every level by differentiation, self-organization, and communion[2]. "Every level," means all creation, all life, all species, and individual organisms like you and me.

As we grow from infant to child to adult, we increasingly direct our personal evolution with self-aware consciousness—consciousness intertwined with multiple interpersonal relationships involving others and shifting interior relationships involving different aspects of ourselves.

Humans are social beings. We are conceived in physical and energetic union with mother, born into families and tribes, and eventually identify with likeminded groups. Conscious awareness blossoms as language and knowledge of past/present/future comes online through our first two years.[3] Deep within our sense of self is a yearning to return to harmonious unity through integration of the differentiated aspects of interior and interpersonal existence. This yearning informs every spiritual path, yogic practice, relationship, and compassionate act.

Therapy is all about relationships. Our lives are dominated by interpersonal relationships, relationships with thousands of aspects of the world around us, and interior relationships with countless aspects of ourselves, including shifting states of consciousness. States of consciousness can have body memories, beliefs, emotional memories, and impulses to act in certain ways—everything constantly in motion and happening simultaneously in the past, present, and future.[4]

Relationships can be more or less healthy, and that's where therapy comes in. Therapists support healthy integration of *intra*personal and *inter*personal relationships, and the direction of that integration is toward wider embrace, more compassionate understanding, and unity with all.

Don calls a therapist.

Consider the following exchange between Don, a forty-four year old insurance executive, and Dr. Theo Brown, a fifty-nine year old psychologist Don has called to inquire about scheduling a session. The italicized sections represent interior thoughts:

> Don: *"I told her I'd call. Just dial the damn number. Nancy said she'd leave if we didn't get therapy."* He dials, it rings, and someone picks up.
>
> Theo: "Hello, Dr. Brown speaking."
>
> Don: "I'm calling about coming in with my wife."
>
> Theo: *"He sounds stressed. Suicidal? Probably was an effort to call."* "Sure, we can make an appointment if you'd like. Do you have any questions you'd like to ask me?"
>
> Don: *"Tell him. Nancy insisted."* "Well, it has to do with an affair. Have you had any experience helping people with affairs?"
>
> Theo: *"Open this up just a little. Who's involved? Is it still happening?"* He laughs briefly. *"Thousands of times. Don't exaggerate."* "Yes, literally hundreds of times. Is it you or your partner that's having the affair?"
>
> Don: A little flustered being so direct, but relieved to be talking about what's dominating his life right now. "Well, it's over now. I ended it. I was involved with another woman and my wife Nancy found out about it. Now we need to save our marriage."

There are dozens of relationships revealed here. The obvious ones are Don's with Theo, Nancy, and his lover, but there are many others. Don is also relating to the part of himself that that doesn't want to call the therapist, the Don that feels coerced by Nancy to call, and the Don who wants to save his marriage. Some combination of all these relationships has resulted in Don's decision. Conflicts between such interior parts generate confusion, create distress, and block awareness, change, and healthy integration.

Dr. Theo Brown is relating to Don, his wife, lover, possible children, and various interior aspects of himself including the Theo who is threatened by Don's potential for self-destruction, the Theo who wants to help, and the Theo who feels compassionate responsibility to evaluate Don's potential for violence to himself or others. Organizing Theo's attention is his intention to serve the highest good.

All of these relationships can be considered from multiple perspectives—perspectives influenced by aspects of each person's body/mind/spirit in self/culture/nature[5].

Don and Theo's exchange reflects some of the many relationships that will be explored in this book. People constantly shift selves, enter different states of consciousness, and yearn for homeostatic balance with numerous internal and external forces. Each moment can be more or less healthy, and more or less consciously available to our executive ego—the core sense of self we choose to put in charge.

How effective we are depends upon depth of consciousness, maturity on a variety of developmental lines, and current extent of compassionate understanding of ourselves and others. Therapy cultivates these attributes and supports integration of clients' interpersonal and intrapersonal selves toward unity.

Therapy from the inside and outside of clients and therapists.

If you are a therapist, you know how hard it is to translate what is taught about psychotherapy into "What do I do now?" in the session. I think this is partially because therapists, perhaps more than any other profession, have to have coherent, conscious relationships with a wide variety of their inner selves to be consistently effective in sessions. Attending to shifting states and perspectives happening simultaneously in the past, present, and future is difficult to describe, much less teach.

A popular local marriage and family therapist once told me that he didn't know quite what to do in individual sessions. In retrospect, he was resisting addressing his clients' conflicted intrapersonal relationships with the parts of themselves they tried to hide and avoid, often called "the shadow" because it's routinely hard for us to perceive and acknowledge conflicted or repulsive personal characteristics. Not surprisingly, this reflected his own difficulties with shadow material—difficulties that eventually led to him losing his license and spending years in prison.

Blind spots.

Not attending to inner relationships creates and maintains blind spots that can result in harm. Cultivating a lifestyle that regularly attends to inner relationships (and especially relationships with our shadow aspects) supports health and development. This is especially important for therapists. Cultivating awareness of networks of interior and interpersonal relationships, helping to heal injured ones, and supporting healthy ones is what psychotherapy does. This activity is driven by yearnings for compassionate acceptance of self and hunger for fulfilling love with others.

Many of us have been in therapy, or are interested observers who know the magic that can happen in a session. Discovery, drama, insight, confusion, transformation, and frustration arise out of the alchemy of client and therapist pursuing truth and health while in constantly morphing relationships with aspects of themselves, each other, lovers, family, friends, and all their combined perspectives and environments.

As a client, this pursuit always involves a conscious self—the "I" that looks out at the world through our eyes—relating consciously and unconsciously to others and ourselves.

Families are windows to development, conflict and healing.

The family is the crucible in which we are first fused, eventually separated from, and finally reintegrated into. This book reflects psychotherapeutic theories and practices that support family relationships moving toward unity, and illustrates them by following one family in distress through a series of sessions.

The clients in this book are fictitious, but are typical of families and individuals who enter therapy. The therapists are also fictitious, but typical of experienced therapists.

Beautiful, Good, and True

We are drawn to what feels moral, practical, and reasonably attractive. These are the three validity standards our nervous systems are programmed to bring to bear on most decisions. Philosophers from Plato to Kant to Habermas have referred to these standards as, "the beautiful, good, and true."[6]

I first encountered the beautiful, good, and true while studying the writings of Ken Wilber[7], who synthesized and built on multiple approaches to develop his Integral model. This model asserts that reality is best understood as happening simultaneously from multiple perspectives, with the central five being the interiors and exteriors of individuals and groups, developmental lines and levels, states of consciousness, and types of individual.

Drawing from voluminous sources, Wilber has observed how humans experience the world from "I," "we," and "it" points of view. "I" can be attracted or repulsed by any part of my environment, "we" can have shared understanding, and "it"—or "its"—involves dealing with all things as objects.

Inherent in the "I" perspective is the "beautiful," which includes the aesthetic—what "I" subjectively find appealing or not. The "we" perspective includes the moral—what "we" collectively and subjectively have shared values about. The "true" includes the scientific—what is objectively observable and verifiable. Our nervous systems are hard wired to bring these three validity standards to bear on our experience.[8] They figure hugely in the practice of psychotherapy, since people will be less trusting of new perspectives or behaviors if they seem invalid by even one validity standard.

Yum and yuck

The beautiful, good, and true form a background hum to life. Each can stand out when something feels especially beautiful or repulsive, good or bad, or true or untrue. We'll notice this spike by a "yum" or "yuck" reaction that moves us in some fashion.

I might be breathless with delight at the sight of a beautiful painting, or close my eyes in repulsion at an ugly caricature.

We may find ourselves moved to tears at the moral compassion of the Dalai Lama or Martin Luther King, or be morally outraged by an executive looting his company's pension fund.

A study that shows vitamin D levels being associated with decreased risk of some forms of cancer might draw our interested attention, while we may dismiss an assertion that harsher sentences for drug abusers reduce use when we discover it has no statistically valid basis.

Yum and yuck are useful access points to our beautiful, good, and true reactions to life experiences. Since therapy always generally supports helping people embrace new perspectives and make healthy discernments and decisions, yum and yuck play prominent roles in sessions.

The beautiful is all about "I"

The "beautiful" is what subjectively attracts or repels—which is apparent in art appreciation where "I know what I like" is understood by most. The beautiful validity standard is individual, interior, and idiosyncratic (people often have different opinions about what is attractive or repulsive). An oil derrick might look like an exquisite engineering marvel, or like an ugly blot on nature. *Pulp Fiction* was my favorite movie one year, while *The Little Mermaid* was my daughter's. This information is internally verifiable. I hear a song, taste a dish, read a poem, or see an image, and it attracts or repulses me. The beautiful validity standard is individual, subjective, interior, and is all about "I".

The beautiful is central to therapy. Here's an example of it in the phone exchange between Don and Dr. Theo Brown:

Theo: "Is this your first time in therapy?"
Don: *"It's so weak to ask for help."* He responds to Theo with a self-deprecating tone. It's clearly ugly, not beautiful, to

him to ask for this kind of help. "I've never had to do this before."

Theo: *"He probably feels weak and unattractive being overwhelmed like this. Support him."* "I think it's a courageous and beautiful thing to ask for therapy to save your marriage."

Don: Embarrassed, but pleased. "Well, uh, thank you."

The good is all about "we"

The "good" is what seems right or wrong, moral or immoral. It is a subjective, shared, moral sense that we consciously and/or unconsciously use to make judgments about ourselves and others. We're driving to the store and see someone injured by the side of the road. It feels "good" or "right" to stop and help. It feels "bad" or "wrong" to do nothing. The good is institutionalized in the laws and customs of cultures. It is now illegal in France to not help someone in dire immediate need. You and I might not agree on what is good, but we will each have an internal sense of what is good or bad, may assume it is a shared sense with others, and will tend to make judgments if we perceive moral violations. The good is subjective, interior—sensed within and collectively—an is all about "we."

The good is always a subtext of psychotherapy, and it appears quickly in Theo and Don's conversation:

Theo: *"How available is his wife to therapy?"* "Is your wife willing to come into therapy with you?"

Don: Feeling a sinking sensation of being caught doing something horribly wrong. Remembering his wife, Nancy, raging at him last night. "She said I'd have to leave if we didn't get therapy, but she also said she'll never forgive me, and that this is the worst thing I could do to her."

Theo: *"Self-flagellation. A relational pattern of his passive aggressive mistakes and her moral condemnations? Plant seeds."* "Did it violate your personal principles to have an affair?"

Don: Surprised. *"Principles?* "Of course I don't think it's right to cheat on my wife."

Theo: Attuning to Don with a shared moral value. "That's a good thing. It suggests therapy for you will partly be about being more true to your own principles."

Don: Feeling a surprising sense of relief. "I suppose so."

The true is all about "it" and "its"

The "true" is what is externally verifiable, what science can tell us empirically through direct observation of individuals and statistical representation of groups. Science deals with observable, measurable phenomena. "True" data about you includes what color your eyes are, how tall you are, how much you weigh, and what your blood pressure is at this moment. If your name is Emily and you announce, "My name is Emily," everyone listening will probably agree, and audiotape would provide confirmation. This is externally verifiable data where everything observed (such as an apple, a table, a dog, a sunset, or an Emily) is observed as an "it."

Groups and systems observed from the outside can generate objective data. Smokers have a higher risk of lung cancer, regular aerobic exercise reduces heart attack risk, and groups in crisis tend to initially support each other for the first twenty-four hours after being traumatized. If there is doubt, additional observations can be made on similar groups to see if they react the same.

Externally verifiable, replicable results are the gold standard of science and constitute the "true" validity standard. The true deals with all phenomena as objects that can be externally observed and objectively represented. Thus the "true" is objective, exterior, individual or collective, and is all about "it" and "its".

Psychotherapists are taught to use "true" data to help their clients remediate symptoms, enhance health, and support development. Here it appears in the phone conversation with Theo and Don:

Don: *"What's the use? Nancy said she hates me and will never forgive me."* "Does it even make sense for us to come in? Do couples ever recover from affairs like this?"

Theo: Quoting scientifically verifiable data. "Over half the couples who come to me with affairs like this, and who want to save their marriages, do stay together. In fact, such couples usually report being closer and more satisfied after therapy than before the affair." Don audibly sighs in relief. These are much better odds than he has been assuming. He relaxes and spends a few minutes filling Theo in about his family and his current situation.

The beautiful, good, and true validity standards are consciously and unconsciously brought to bear on almost everything, and harmonize with the many yums and yucks of life. They are vital to psychotherapy because clients need to feel therapist input is consistent with scientific research (true), attractive as alternative perspectives and actions (beautiful), and moral according to each client's principles (good). The therapeutic relationship is based on the client's continuing trust that the therapist's perspectives and actions meet all three validity standards.

Therapy is helping clients make discernments and decisions that seem beautiful, good, and true, and that guide them to becoming more healthy and productive. Any decision that doesn't meet one of these standards usually benefits from deeper consideration.

One of the great strengths of healthy intimate relationships is that couples have access to each other's beautiful, good, and true standards. This synergy gives each the benefit of their partner's input and also opens up the door to receiving personal feedback from others in general. Others often have more clarity about us than we have about ourselves—especially in areas where we are conflicted, defended, or confused.

How does psychotherapy address basic needs for meaning and purpose?

We often find meaning and purpose by orienting to perspectives, goals, and actions that are "yums" to us, and then directing—or allowing—ourselves to honor those perspectives, embrace those goals, and engage in those actions. This involves harmonizing relationships between the parts of us that direct/allow and the parts that are directed/allowed.

The purpose of psychotherapy, what therapists organize the culture of each therapy session around, is helping clients remediate symptoms, enhance health, and support development by cultivating understanding of themselves and others—depth of consciousness—while always reaching for and offering their best sense of what is in the highest good for all—compassion. Not surprisingly, compassionate understanding is usually the most accurate understanding, and is likely to result in yums.

Six processes therapists use to help are relating, teaching, inspiring, confronting, interpreting, and directing in accordance with their own and their client's validity standards.[9]

In the above phone conversation, Dr. Theo Brown and Don were cocreating a healing culture in which Theo was supporting compassion, depth of consciousness, and healthy perspectives and actions on Don's part. Theo's goals were to remediate symptoms, enhance health, and support development in Don and everybody affiliated with Don. He was pursuing those goals by attuning to himself and Don with caring intent, teaching Don about the therapeutic process, inspiring him to reach for resolution of problems and healthier perspectives, confronting his distorted beliefs about therapy, interpreting this situation as a healing process, and directing him how to deal with his current catastrophic situation.

Masculine and Feminine

My favorite teacher of the principles of masculine/feminine aspect and essence is David Deida. He maintains that all people have unique combinations of masculine and feminine aspects, and that most individuals in their deepest heart have a more masculine or more feminine essence. This deepest essence informs us in creating our personal identities, guides us on our developmental paths, supports understanding in dealing with the world, dramatically influences intimate relationships, and provides insight into life purpose.

Goals of psychotherapy include helping people know themselves, develop well, deal effectively with life challenges, have more secure and loving interior and interpersonal attachments, and be true to fundamental principles and life missions. Knowing how to support deepest masculine or feminine sexual essence—and helping harmonize masculine and feminine aspects—serves these goals.

The masculine craves emptiness, freedom, feminine radiance, deep purpose, and meaning at the edge of death.

Masculine people tend to be happiest when they have satisfying feminine warmth and erotic radiance, work that feels deeply meaningful, and personal passions that nourish them with the sense of being on the edge of death (like sports, professional striving, or risk taking). The masculine gift is deepest consciousness—compassionate understanding of self, others, and the world—expressed in healing agency by identifying and solving problems—or, as Deida puts it, turning somethings into nothings[10]. The fundamental masculine question is, "Am I being true to my deepest purpose?" Masculine people suffer when they violate their own principles, feel a loss of—or threat to—freedom, collapse in the face of stress, are deprived of feminine radiance, or are unresolved as to what best serves the moment.

Masculine qualities that attract the feminine are being present, standing unrecoiling in the face of threat or challenge, having deep understanding (depth of consciousness, especially about her), a sense of humor, and understanding, containing, and utilizing the power of his dark side—shadow. Shadow includes those aspects of self such as our violent or socially unacceptable beliefs and impulses that we have trouble perceiving and acknowledging. A central masculine drive is toward freedom. A central masculine life rhythm is success, failure, success, failure, and so on until death.

The feminine craves love, fullness, masculine presence, and communion with all.

Feminine people are happy when they feel themselves radiant wellsprings of love and light, and love is happening satisfactorily.

They are healthiest when they can be current and open with their emotions, have daily pleasure in the body, feel known and claimed by their masculine partner, and are free to express pleasure and suffering. The feminine gives as compassionate caring, holding without agenda. The fundamental feminine question is, "Is love being served?" Feminine people suffer when they block emotion, hold on to old pain, adapt to people or situations out of fear or anger, and when love is not being served.

Aspects of the feminine that tend to attract the masculine are warmth and feminine erotic radiance. A central feminine drive is toward love. A central feminine life rhythm is love is happening, love is not happening, love is happening, love is not happening, and so on until death.[11]

The following exchange between Don and his lover, Denise, reflects a variety of masculine/feminine aspects and dynamics. It is a late summer afternoon, and they are driving in his Mercedes up the California Coastline north of Santa Barbara. The ocean is on their left and rolling hills rising into chaparral covered mountains are on their right. This area is where they've had many of their most romantic trysts, so discussing separation here is particularly heartbreaking. Denise is thirty-three, blond, radiant, and dressed in a pink pastel sundress that makes Don ache with desire to touch her and love her. Don is in his business suit, haggard and stressed. He's in so much pain over the potential loss of his family that he's somewhat separate—empathetically disconnected from—the devastation this breakup means to Denise, who has been imagining Don as her life partner since they became lovers a year ago:

> Denise: *"How could he go back to her? All she does is trash him and use him. I love him.* She starts to cry. "How can you go back to her? You don't love her. You love me. She doesn't love you, she owns you."
>
> Don: Smelling her jasmine scent and hungering for her. *"Denise, I love you so much, baby. I'm such an idiot. I'm so sorry.* "I can't do this to my kids. I've got to try to save the family. I'm so sorry."

Denise: *"He really means it. It will never work with her. I love him, she uses him."* She unconsciously turns up the power of her feminine light, turning to him and opening her heart. "It won't work and you'll come back to me."

Don: Unconsciously leaning in towards her, as the power of her devotional love and erotic radiance draw his attention magnetically. Speaking miserably. "I'm sorry. It's just not right for my kids. Our relationship has never been right for them. I should have left Nancy before we became involved."

Denise: *"I'd be a better mother than that bitch. She's so cold."* "You told me yourself she fights with the kids all the time. Leave her now. The kids will eventually get used to it. They like me, I played video games with Michael for an hour at the office party."

Don: Resolved. "No. I've been selfish being with you. I have to see if I can salvage my family. Nancy loves the kids and they love her. We are a family and I've screwed up. We're going to try therapy, and you should too. The therapist I talked to gave me some names you can call."

Denise: Instantly suspicious. *"Did Don make me out to be some kind of nut case?"* "Why? What did you tell him about me?"

Don: *"I knew she'd be mad if I suggested it, but Dr. Brown said it was a good idea."* "He said this is going to be hard for you because we're used to supporting each other and we can't have contact if we break up. I'm worried about you, and I'd feel better if you were getting help and support from a good person."

Paradoxically, the more resolve Don demonstrates to save his family in spite of his obvious hunger for Denise, the more attractive he becomes to her. He is standing up for his principles. Denise unconsciously is using her feminine powers of yearning for love to pull him back. Ironically, if he ignored his values and surrendered to her, he would eventually become less attractive because of his collapse. Love being served is Denise's feminine organizing principle, so it is emotionally almost incomprehensible to her that he would choose duty over love. Meanwhile, Don is willing to sacrifice the most passionate love of his life for duty (a masculine principle), and is having trouble understanding why this doesn't make sense to Denise.

The masculine and feminine often live in different worlds.

This book presents principles, techniques, and perspectives of psychotherapy while following Don, Nancy, Denise and Don and Nancy's two children through sessions with Theo and other therapists. We'll observe their myriad relationships and how they are highlighted, brought to consciousness, and worked with in and out of therapy to move each person toward greater harmony and unity.

Endnotes

[1] de Chardin (1959)
[2] Swimme (1992)
[3] Witt (2007)
[4] Siegel (1999)
[5] Wilber (2007)
[6] Wilber (1995)
[7] Wilber (1995)
[8] Siegel (1999)
[9] Witt (2008)
[10] Deida (2006)
[11] *Ibid*

CHAPTER ONE

Relationships with Self and Others

Narcissus glances in the glass
and smiles in satisfaction.
He will shine throughout the night
The center of attraction.

Bipolar Di is on her high,
ready to meet Jesus.
He slightly nods, amid applause
Sick enough to believe it.

Then all at once it all blows up
in flaming, screaming faces.
Narcissus takes her by the hand
and spins her till she's senseless
Her sister's giving him the eye
while Shakespeare's cruising Elvis.

Make you, shake you,
Any way they take you
at the Borderline Ball tonight.
~from *Borderline Ball*~

In 1975 a Transactional Analysis therapist named Denton Roberts began doing training and supervision with our staff at the Family Education and Counseling Center in Goleta, Ca. Transactional Analysis is a psychotherapeutic approach developed by Eric Berne who maintained that how we relate to ourselves and others is the driving force of human existence, health, pathology, and psychotherapy. Denton was invited to work with us by my colleague Dr. Lynne Cantlay who seemed to have a knack for finding great therapists and theorists to teach, supervise, and support the staffs of the two counseling centers that she, Steve Aizenstadt, Ken Fishman, myself, and others had founded in 1974. Denton was an amazing man. A real cowboy from Wyoming, he was the minister at All Peoples Church in L.A, operated a pack station with his family in the High Sierra, was the father of two boys, ran T.A. groups out of his church, and was flat out one of the best therapists I'd ever met.

Denton and I took our Marriage Family Counseling oral licensing exam at the same time, and, while the rest of us anxiously paced the examination waiting area, worrying about how to answer questions about the hypothetical cases the oral examiners would present, he—completely relaxed and unattached—said, "Bring the family in and I'll just work with them."

Denton's great gift was that he always maintained a compassionate relationship with different parts of his clients and himself. He seemed to be simultaneously dedicated to serving the highest good of everyone involved in each clinical situation, tuned in relationally with the relevant players, and detached from whatever outcome ensued.

Once a dramatic hostile couple he was working with woke Denton at 1:00 A.M. while they were in the midst of a huge fight. Denton felt into the situation, realized it was mostly drama, and when the guy fired off a pistol and hung up, Denton went to sleep and called them in the morning. For this particular couple, this was the ideal intervention, and their embarrassment the next day help propel them into more ability self-regulate their capacities for toxic drama. By today's risk management standards, going to sleep and calling them in the morning was a reckless and foolish thing for Denton to do, but feeling into the situation and trusting his attunements with himself and his clients, it turned out to be a healing intervention.

Cultivating compassionate relationships with all aspects of yourself and others is what therapy does. But what exactly does this mean? Who is relating to whom? In the above story, at 1:00 the angry impulsive aspects of the man and wife were engaged in negative drama while disconnected from their more mature selves. They were lost in defensive states of consciousness where they had amplified emotions, distorted beliefs and perceptions, destructive impulses, and reduced capacities for self-reflection and empathy.

Denton, abruptly woken up by their negative drama, was initially alarmed and irritated, but reflexively acknowledged and soothed his distress and reached for compassion. If he had gone to sleep and not called the couple back because he was angry and disgusted, it would have been an irresponsible act (likely to result in harm for everyone). Doing the same from compassionate understanding was an inspired intervention.

The next day the husband and wife, disengaged from their defensive states and in states of healthy response to the present moment, came in embarrassed by their drama. They now believed in their capacity for loving connection, and were somewhat puzzled by the previous night's behavior. Gratefully responding to Denton's compassion and understanding, they were motivated to learn and grow from their mistakes. Where were these states of healthy response to the present moment the previous night? Why can't we always access states of healthy response? Why can't we always create secure, loving connections with our intimates?

Defensive states and states of healthy response to the present moment.

There are myriad states of consciousness that we shift in and out of constantly. There are meditative states, peak experiences, regressed states, and altered states as a result of drugs, disease, injury, or environmental restimulations. Each of these has interior, subjective characteristics (such as love, joy, interest, boredom, shame, hatred, or transcendent unity), and exterior, objectively measurable characteristics (such as non-verbal signals, endocrine activity, altered brainwaves, or physiological arousal).

David Deida's teachings assert that we are either opening the moment by doing our best to do right and serve others, or closing the moment by surrendering to immature or egocentric impulses that cause harm to ourselves and others.[1] These reflect two classes of states, one group which is attuned to optimally serve self and others right now, and one which is not.

Psychotherapists have always observed that clients are either more open to change and growth, or more in the grip of defensive resistance. Clients more open to change and growth are in states of healthy response to the present moment. Clients who resist change and growth are often being influenced by defensive states—habits of amplified or numbed emotions, distorted perspectives and thoughts, destructive impulses, and reduced capacities for self-reflection and empathy.[2]

States of healthy response to the present moment involve attunement.

Healthy responses to the present moment generally involve us being attuned to ourselves and others. Attunement involves feeling into ourselves and others with caring intent.[3] Sometimes healthy attuned states are automatic. We see a stop sign, stop our car, look both ways, and proceed. Our wife says "Good morning", and kisses us, and we say "Good morning" back and return the kiss. It's time for work, and we go to work. We become hungry, so we eat healthy food. It's late and we're tired, so we go to bed.

Sometimes we have to reach for attunement. A father notices he's angry with his defiant four-year-old son, feels like yelling at him, but instead tells himself that his son is hungry and had no nap today, and deals with him compassionately rather than punitively. A healthy response to the present moment is a state of consciousness where we cultivate the best approach we can—depending upon our knowledge and maturity—that serves the highest good. Defensive states are another thing entirely.

Defensive states start young and echo throughout life.

Most of our defensive states became established when we were infants, toddlers, and small children. We learned to protect ourselves from threat by developing habits of fleeing from—or attacking—what threatened us either externally (like an angry, condemning parent) or internally (like a forbidden thought or fantasy).

Such learning continues throughout development. An eighteen month old is frightened of her raging mother and becomes numb and distant when screamed at. An older brother is mean to a four-year-old who might run from the room, yell out protests, surrender, attack, or seek a safe other—usually a parent—to come to the rescue. A five-year-old girl makes a mistake, feels guilty, ashamed, or embarrassed, and might make excuses, blame someone else, forget about it quickly, or hide. These are natural responses of children to intrapersonal and interpersonal stress. If such states are entered repetitively, they can become habits that persist and become permanent defensive structures. When cued by perceived threat, defensive structures *automatically and unconsciously* kick in to protect us.

Yes, *automatically* and *unconsciously*. If we don't cultivate enough depth of consciousness to be *aware* of these defenses, and enough compassion to *care for* ourselves and others while we're in these states, we will automatically do damage to ourselves and/or others without consciously noticing that we've shifted from a state of healthy response to a defensive state.

Intrapersonally, defensive states reflect injured or pathological relationships between threatened parts of ourselves and our observing ego—the more or less conscious part of us that is in charge of our will and can direct our attention, intention, and behavior. Our observing ego can be underdeveloped, injured, or fused with distressed inner aspects, and thus struggle to be aware of defensive states, and resist reaching for attunement.

Worse, since we are energetically connected to people around us in interlocking networks of intersubjective fields, when we enter a defensive state, everyone around us will feel varying levels of impulse to enter complementary defensive states. This is one example of how indulging defensive states closes the moment for everybody. When two or more of us enter reciprocal defensive states we are mutually supporting unhealthy defensive patterns, manifesting relational defensive structures that become progressively more reflexive and urgent the more we indulge them. Secure interpersonal attachment can be enormously difficult under these circumstances.[4] This is where problems arise and solidify in relationships with family members, lovers, children, and friends.

So, if we're regularly shifting from one state of consciousness to another, who are we?

The observing ego.

The "I" that looks out through our eyes at the world is our observing ego. This "I" has two main components; the unchanging self that feels the same from birth to death, and the ever changing self that continues to grow, adapt and adjust to different circumstances each day of our life.

What is your earliest memory? Are you an infant, a toddler, or a small child? Are you by yourself or with another person? There is a flavor of you in that memory that is exactly the same flavor of you as you read this paragraph. This unchanging "I" is what David Deida calls the masculine aspect in all of us.[5]

On the other hand, you probably have very different opinions about the world right now than you did ten, twenty, or thirty years ago (or perhaps ten, twenty, or thirty minutes ago). If you screamed at your dog this morning for chewing up the couch, you might look at your adorable dog now, feel a flood of affection and guilt, and think, *"How could I have screamed at you?"* You were in a defensive state this morning of amplified or numbed emotion (you just bought the couch and it enraged you to see it torn), distorted perspectives and beliefs (your dog should have known better, he probably deliberately chewed up the couch for some selfish dog reason), and destructive impulses (you wanted to hit him, and screaming seemed like an appropriate response).

All our shifting states of consciousness reflect the ever changing "I" that Deida calls our feminine aspect; in contact with the world, immersed in experience and change, shifting from state to state, perspective to perspective.[6]

Sexual polarity.

Our deepest sexual essence automatically creates energetic polarities with the deepest sexual essences of the people in our environment. Americans tend to be both overly fascinated with sexual issues, and overly judgmental and frightened of sexual issues; you could say we are both sexaphilic and sexaphobic.

Sexual attraction and arousal in couples (heterosexual and homosexual) almost universally happens between one partner in a more masculine moment and the other partner in a more feminine moment.

More masculine people will be drawn to feminine radiance, and more feminine people will be drawn to masculine power, presence and depth of consciousness. When in proximity to each other, masculine and feminine individuals naturally tend to create intersubjective energy arcs of polarity.

Polarity is not confined to arcs of energy between masculine and feminine individuals, since energetic polarities constellate between us and everything/everyone we relate to. Sometimes polarity is experienced as overtly sexual, and sometimes it is not. Polarity constellates between different people, between individuals and objects (a skier feeling energetic polarity with the fresh powder on his run), or between an individual and other living beings (a girl feeling energetic polarity with her horse).

Our "good" validity standard can subtly pathologize sexual feelings that therapists might have during sessions. Given that all masculine people have some level of sexual polarity with all feminine people (and vice versa), this has led to a lot of problems over the years. Sexual polarity does not necessarily mean that two individuals are sexually aroused, or even attracted. Sexual polarity means that the energetic relationships between a more masculine person and a more feminine person, between two more masculine people, or between two more feminine people are different kinds of energetic relationships that feel different and operate according to different principles.

Polarity as a therapeutic tool.

Good therapists often deliberately and/or instinctively use their inner experiences and their observations of their clients as guides to discerning the different polarities in the session. Confrontation in therapy is often simply the therapist telling the client his best understanding of such polarities.

Denton once told a woman named Sally in a group he was leading that he was feeling a sexual tingle as she spoke. Sally, a little taken aback, denied radiating any sexual energy and assumed the confrontation was some aspect of "Denton's material" (his own unresolved conflicts). Years later Sally discovered she had a defense of dissociating from her feminine erotic radiance, and would put out, even feel, sexual energies without being consciously aware of them. Denton never found out that his confrontation eventually percolated through Sally's defenses to become healing insight in support of her health and growth. He felt the erotic polarity, normalized it with compassionate understanding, felt Sally's dissociation, and offered a confrontation believing, as most therapists do, that bringing unconscious material to conscious awareness is generally a healing activity. When Sally didn't receive it as useful feedback, that was fine with him, and he moved on in the session, unafraid of his sexuality, Sally's sexuality, or the sexual polarity that he—but not she—consciously felt between them.

Energetic polarities, and especially sexual polarities, permeate our lives. We will explore polarity more deeply in Chapter Four.

The abilities to stand unrecoiling in the face of anything, and to hold and care without agenda.

Denton's capacity to be calmly accepting of a possible embarrassing error (he could have been either wrong in his perception, or unwise in offering the confrontation) reflected a core characteristic of a trustable masculine presence, the ability to stand unrecoiling in the face of anything in service of love. His capacity to feel compassion and caring for himself and Sally—independent of any certain understanding of what was going on—reflected a core characteristic of feminine healing; holding and caring without agenda or demand. Good therapists, no matter what their deepest sexual essence, usually give freely from both their masculine and feminine aspects, depending upon the demands of the moment.

Denton's genius was his ability to discern healthy from defensive states, to never allow his defensive states to dictate his thoughts or actions, and to instinctively reach for compassionate perspectives that served the highest good. When I was around him he consistently seemed to have compassionate understanding of himself and others, and to be organized around caring for everybody in ways that supported each of us. All this made him a natural healing presence. In a healthy moment, you felt his recognition and approval, and if you were in a defensive moment, you were pulled towards healthier perspectives by his compassion, depth of consciousness, sense of humor, and genuine desire to help.

I've observed many great therapists from many traditions in my career, and have been dazzled by their knowledge, expertise, and charisma. What they have had in common is their capacities to be caring, genuinely authentic, self-aware, and self-regulating.

As I introduce the clients and therapists that we'll be following throughout this book, you'll observe their different healthy and defensive states of consciousness, the interplay of their masculine and feminine aspects, their *intra*personal relationships with different parts of themselves, and *inter*personal relationships with others. In the sessions, you'll see the therapists help integrate these aspects and relationships by cultivating compassion and depth of consciousness in themselves and their clients to support healthy perspectives and actions, always organized around helping clients remediate symptoms, enhance health, and support development. This process naturally moves toward wider embrace and deeper understanding—in the direction of unity.

Attunement does not just happen interpersonally between intimates, but also intrapersonally between various interior aspects of ourselves. When we attune with conflicting parts of ourselves, we heal historic wounds and integrate toward more mature caring. Similarly, when we extend attunement to others, we help heal old wounds and repair current wounds by maintaining states of consciousness that sustain healthy responses in ourselves while supporting and evoking healthy responses in them.[7]

Endnotes

[1] Deida (2004)
[2] Witt (2008)
[3] Witt (2007)
[4] Siegel (2003)
[5] Deida (1997)
[6] *Ibid*
[7] Witt (2007)

CHAPTER TWO

All good people

Don't believe when you feel insane
That you're to blame
For all their pain,
Just breathe and see it through,
Good people can see it through.

Just remember they're all good people
All good people, all good people,
Don't you know that they're all good people,
All good people, all good people.

~from, All Good People~

Let's meet Don, Nancy, their children, Denise, Theo, and two other therapists, Mary and Harvey.

We all have a wide range of experiences when encountering new people. Therapists are trained to use their minds and bodies to register huge amounts of information. In therapy, a client walks into the room and data starts flooding through all the therapist's channels. Initially over 70% of this data is non-verbal. How does the client look, sound, smell, move, and breathe? What feelings, thoughts, memories, or associations are evoked in the therapist by the presence of the client? Through observation and conversation, much more information flows into the session. Current functioning, vocation, age, physical health and infirmity, medication, drug and alcohol use, family history, personal narrative, dreams, hopes, and interpersonal/intrapersonal relationships are all important and relevant dimensions.

When a couple or family comes in, the amount of information increases by an order of magnitude as their relationships and polarities are revealed in dialog and non-verbal relating.

Don and Nancy's family is typical of millions of similar families struggling to do right and live the American ideal. Don and Nancy are typical of most humans who want love, and who attract their reciprocals—partners who radiate complementary wounds and dreams:

Don: Forty-four, is third generation Irish, balding, owns an insurance business, and has been married to Nancy for nineteen years. He often seems mildly depressed, but, when relaxed and playful—sometimes under the influence of a couple of drinks—Don can get reckless and raucous. Twenty pounds overweight, he works out at the gym two times a week, and loves his weekly tennis match. Don can appear mature and attractive (mostly with Denise), weak and indecisive or, very occasionally, angry and intimidating. Raised in Southern California's Orange County, he is the youngest of three children, and is still close to his two older sisters and their families. Don was an underachiever from childhood through college but, when he discovered that being a successful businessman was deeply important and satisfying, built a thriving insurance business through committing himself to high standards at work and then showing up every day. Don enjoyed playing high school football, and likes to watch sports on T.V.

A year ago he and his office manager Denise began an affair, which has resulted in the most romantically passionate involvement of his life. In recent years, Don has come to believe his marriage is emotionally and sexually barren, and this was the main rational for his affair. Generally he is his best self around Denise: in charge, caring, fun loving, and with an endearing sense of humor. He is often closed, defensive, and passive-aggressive around Nancy.

Don's family of origin (the family he grew up in) was generally supportive of the children, was non-expressive emotionally, and hid problems, especially problems between his parents who divorced when he was fifteen. Don's mother is still a practicing alcoholic whose drinking began accelerating when Don was in sixth grade. His weekly "check in" calls are on Sunday morning to catch her sober. Don has always been contemptuous of therapy because he thinks it's weak to ask for emotional help, and fearful of therapy because he unconsciously assumes it is a place he will discover negative things or, worse, a place he will be hammered and pathologized by a credible professional in the same way he is by Nancy when she's angry.

Don was raised Presbyterian, but rarely goes to church. In stress he occasionally prays, and has some faint hope that there is a God who hears him.

In the following exchange, he's gotten home to his Spanish Style house near the beach on the Mesa in Santa Barbara. The night air is soft, with an on-shore breeze that smells of the ocean and jasmine (which painfully reminds him of Denise).

> Nancy: Hurt, angry, and suspicious, she is cleaning the kitchen as he walks in. "Where were you?"
>
> Don: Shocking both of them by telling the truth. "I took a drive with Denise and told her we had to break up."
>
> Nancy: This is confusing. She feels pleasure that he's telling the truth, relief that he is breaking up, and furious he was with Denise. She starts to cry. "I don't know if I can stand this. I'm glad you broke up, I hate it you were with her."
>
> Don: He is more drawn to her as she shows her suffering talking about her personal experience than when she attacks him. This is generally true for masculine people. "I knew you'd hate it, but I had to tell her in person, and I'm not going to lie anymore."
>
> Nancy: Attracted by his integrity but frightened of surrendering to trust. *"I do love him, but how could he cheat on me?"* "How can I ever trust you again?"

Nancy: Forty-one, is third generation French/Portuguese, with dark brown hair. She is a full-time housewife, and has an existence filled with family responsibilities, exercise, friends, and community involvement. Nancy takes care of herself with diet, yoga, and enthusiastic participation in tennis and working out at the gym. She is compulsive, opinionated, and somewhat rigid if she feels emotionally challenged. During the school year she is busy with volunteer work at eleven-year-old Michael's elementary school. She fights often with hostile, depressed, moderately overweight fifteen-year-old Julie, but blames this entirely on "Julie being a teenager." Nancy has good friends with whom she goes out to dinner and clubs, takes beach and mountain walks, and generally shares a woman culture that is subtly contemptuous of men.

Nancy and her younger sister Ruth were raised in Santa Barbara by perfectionist parents who, to this day, insist that they have the "best family ever." Nancy and Ruth still struggle to earn their parents' approval, which has never seemed to come in completely satisfying ways. The family attended a Baptist church, but Nancy stopped going as a teen, and yoga and psychic readings are the closest she currently gets to spiritual practice. Her parents are still together and seem to like their life. They have never seemed erotically charged, and have not been particularly interested in participating in their grandkids' lives.

Nancy is comfortable when she is accomplishing things, guilty when she is not. She does not take much time for pleasure in the body, or purely pleasurable self-nourishment, and has for years been vaguely hostile toward sex with Don, though she loves reading about hot relationships in her romance novels. She is very uncomfortable discussing anything negative about herself. She doesn't remember why (or how) sex was hot and frequent with Don until she got pregnant with Julie. Nancy likes to read Nora Roberts, Sue Monk Kidd, spirituality books, and self-help.

Nancy had six therapy sessions with a college counselor after a man cheated on her and then left the summer after her junior year, and she feels experienced and expert in the psychological area. She is dismissive of Don's levels of self-awareness and insight.

The following exchange is between Nancy and fifteen-year-old Julie the morning after Don told her about his breakup conversation with Denise. She's rushing to get the kids ready, drive them to school, and be home in time for her and Don to get to their first conjoint therapy session:

Nancy: As she walks by Julie's filthy bathroom, the mess bothers her, but the smell of mold is intolerable. Julie is standing in front of the mirror, sullen and running late as usual. Nancy is angry, distracted, and obsessing about her marriage. *"Why can't she keep the bathroom clean? I don't need this right now. She's so selfish."* "You have to clean the bathroom before we leave."

Julie: *"She's such a bitch. I look fat in this blouse, but my brown one is in the wash."* Unconsciously enjoying the pleasure of frustrating her mother. "Whatever."

Nancy: *"She never listens. I can't get through to her."* "I don't need this today. Start cleaning the bathroom now."

Julie: *"I hate how I look. I'll wear my black pullover again."* She casually begins to put things away. "Yeah, alright."

Nancy: Suddenly, she has an image of Julie as an adorable, happy third grader who couldn't wait to go to school. *"She's unhappy, and I love her so much. I wish I could help."* "I love you honey. I'm just having a bad morning."

Julie: Surprised and touched, she smiles. "It's OK mom, I'll be done in a minute."

Julie: Fifteen, has brown hair dyed black, a stocky but voluptuous body, and often appears depressed or hostile. She dresses Goth (black clothes and dark makeup), thinks Marilyn Manson is cool, and hangs out with an oppositional Goth crowd who cultivate cynical views regarding the inevitable corruption of institutions, adults, and the world. Julie easily despises her mother and is protective of her father who seems vaguely pathetic to her. This last year she has increased her pot smoking from monthly to three or four times a week, and gets drunk occasionally at sleepover parties. Julie has had intercourse with one boy, but didn't particularly enjoy it. She does enjoy secret masturbation fantasies of being ravished (she thinks "raped", with some shame) by confident, powerful rock star types. Julie occasionally dances hip hop with her friends when they hang out, but her parents disparage the music and there have been some heated arguments about Marilyn Manson.

Julie was a good student and athlete (allowing her mother to dominate much of her life) until the seventh grade when she started becoming oppositional and defiant and was first introduced to the Goth drug culture. Now, she and Nancy fight frequently and easily about almost anything, while Don and Michael try to stay out of it; Don because Nancy will blame him for the problems, and Michael because he's distressed by the emotional violence.

The following exchange is between Julie and eleven-year-old Michael as Nancy hurries to get them to their respective schools before she and Don go to therapy:

Michael: *"Maybe Alex will lend me Mortal Combat. I lent him both my Zelda's."* He glances over at Julie. *"That pimple on her forehead looks so gross."* Knowing his sister, he quickly looks away, but it is too late. Julie, like most feminine people, is exquisitely sensitive to energy, especially critical energy.

Julie: "What are you looking at?"

Michael: *"She caught me. It's not fair. I didn't say anything."* "I didn't say anything."

Julie: "I saw you looking at my forehead. Wait till you have acne. I'll bet your face explodes."

Michael: "Mom, Julie's being mean for no reason. I didn't say anything."

Nancy: Michael's whiney tone catches her obsessing about the upcoming therapy session, hoping her life isn't coming completely unraveled, and secretly thinking that Denise is younger, more beautiful, and sexier than she is. She is irritated at the interruption, and unconsciously mobilizes her kick-ass masculine side. "Be quiet, or both of you walk the rest of the way to school. You know I'll do it."

Both kids shut up.

Michael: Eleven, is a quiet, A/B student who likes to surf, skateboard, and play video games with his friends. Michael seems self-contained and happy with life, but is secretly often lonely at home, and regularly ashamed about his sexual fantasies which involve big-breasted *Penthouse* type women. He just started masturbating this last year, though he's never had an orgasm, and doesn't know what to do with his increasingly powerful sexual feelings. Michael has been playing occasional look, touch, suck, sex games at sleepovers with his best friend Alex. They do it but don't talk about it. He has told no one of these activities or fantasies, and feels guilty while also enjoying them. He has four or five friends, including Alex, with whom he mostly plays violent video games, which Nancy criticizes and Don subtly supports. He unconsciously feels somewhat alienated from his family, but likes kid culture and is popular with students and staff at school. Michael has the most even temperament in the family, and doesn't self-reflect much about interior experience though, in his heart, he wishes there was more warmth and love in his world. He doesn't like the regular family conflict, but is largely content as long as routines are maintained, and the trains keep running on time.

Denise: Thirty-three, is a dedicated office manager who lives alone with her two cats and is crazy about Don. Lushly attractive and erotically radiant, Denise enjoys uninhibited sex and good times with Don. She drinks and occasionally smokes pot with him, but non-alcoholically (she is not biochemically wired for chemical dependence, and has always been able to easily take or leave euphorics). Denise has had a history of bonding with emotionally abusive men—one time a physically abusive man—and believes her yearlong affair with Don has been the best relationship of her life. She sympathizes with him feeling victimized by Nancy, and has secret hopes of having her own family with Don. Though a firm believer in safe sex, she has occasionally "accidentally" allowed unprotected sex with him in their last few encounters.

Denise's parents divorced when she was five and her sister was one. She was molested by her stepfather between eight and ten. The molestation finally stopped when, at ten, she gathered her courage and insisted on living with her biological father, and would go into screaming fits when pressured to visit her mother and stepfather. She—and soon after her sister—never stayed alone with their mother and stepfather again. No one ever explored why. Her only explanation was, "I hate them, I won't go there," and she never told anyone about the molests, even after her stepfather's death six years ago in an auto accident. Her mother is still a self-absorbed, depressed, narcissistic alcoholic, and Denise has nothing to do with her, but occasionally spends time with her biological father who's a drywall contractor in town. He lives in an apartment, smokes pot daily, and has never really grown out of a teen-age lifestyle.

Denise occasionally consults with an astrologer, reads new age spirituality books, and attends new age functions where the pervading ethos is everything is wonderful and magic all the time. She also occasionally attends church at the Calvary Chapel in Santa Barbara.

The following exchange is between her and Dr. Harvey McBride, whom she chose from the list of psychologists Dr. Theo Brown recommended she call:

> Denise: "Hello, I'd like to make an appointment. I was referred to you by Dr. Brown."
>
> Dr. McBride: He knows that the main reason Theo would refer someone to him is that there is a potential conflict of with another client that requires combinations of therapists. Such combinations could involve Theo working with a couple and wanting Harvey to do individual work, or, as is the case here, Theo knowing that working with Denise would hopelessly compromise his work with other clients. *"Sounds like relationship conflicts. Theo's probably handling some drama involving her social system, and she needs individual treatment."* "Of course, let's set it up for this week. Are there any questions you'd like to ask me?"
>
> Denise: *"How can he help? Don's leaving me and that's it."* "Do you think you can help me? My boyfriend's going back to his wife, I'm the office manager at his office, and I don't know what to do."
>
> Dr. McBride: *"She's grieving a breakup with her married boss, and probably having to find another job. The first week is usually a full-on nightmare. Unstable relationships mean there might be some characterological stuff happening. She's clearly feminine. Reassure her."* "It sounds like a lot of stress is peaking right now. It's a good thing that you called. Therapy can't take away all the pain,

but it can help you hurt less and grow more through the tough times. You will feel better. I've helped people with problems like this before."

Denise: Relaxing at his reassuring tone and presence. *"Stress and pain is right. I feel like I want to die. He sounds so solid."* "Thank you, I've just been overwhelmed."

Theo Brown, Ph.D.: Theo is fifty-nine and has been practicing psychotherapy for thirty-six years. He's and his fifty-seven year old wife Sandy have been together since he was in his PhD program. They have three children: a twenty-three year old son in graduate school, a twenty-year-old son in college, and a sixteen-year-old daughter in high school. He and Sandy often take beach walks before work. The following exchange is during a walk they're taking the morning of Don and Nancy's first session:

Theo: "God, I love how the ocean smells in the morning."

Sandy: She smiles, and starts talking about her day, but notices that Theo is distracted. "Is something on your mind?"

Theo: "I'm seeing a new couple today and there's been an affair. I don't know what the deal is yet, but it sounds like it could be explosive."

Sandy: *"He deals with this all the time. What's different?"* "You sound worried."

Theo: *"She's right. What is it about this couple? The wife might be a borderline and the guy certainly sounds passive-aggressive. That's not it. It's the daughter. I hope she's not locked down into some teen self-destruction thing. Maybe she'll see a therapist. Mary West is great with teen girls. I'll call her when we get home."* "I feel solid about the guy, but I haven't met his wife and she sounds like she rages. It's their kids that worry me. I'm concerned about the daughter. You know how teenagers can get screwed when the parents generate negative drama."

Sandy: Confidently. This is the part of her man that is the most solid. "You'll know what to do."

Mary West, MFT: Mary is forty-seven, second generation Japanese, and married with a ten-year-old daughter. She has been a licensed Marriage, Family, and Child Therapist for twenty-two years and often shares referrals with Theo. She happens to be home for his call and, after some friendly civilities, he asks if she's taking new clients:

> Mary: "I have some openings. What's involved?"
>
> Theo: "I don't know yet, exactly. It's a family with two kids, a fifteen-year-old girl and an eleven-year-old boy. I only talked briefly with the father, but the girl might need sessions. She's a Goth."
>
> Mary: She has a sudden vision of two hostile, multiply pierced Goth teens she saw on State Street the previous Saturday. It was a boy and a girl and they both seemed stoned and angry. *"Is she depressed? Is she accessible?"* "Will she even agree to come in?"
>
> Theo: "I didn't go into it with the father, he had a lot of other stuff on his mind. I just want to know you're available."
>
> Mary: Feeling a wave of compassion for all unhappy teens. "Sure, I'd like to help."

Harvey McBride, Ph.D.: Harvey is a licensed psychologist who will work individually and in a therapy group with Denise. He is fiercely dedicated to his practice and feels a sacred sense of responsibility to his clients. Fifty-one and divorced three years with one grown son, Harvey's been living alone since the breakup. He has just ended a six-month relationship with a thirty-seven year old woman, partially because she was desperate to have children, but mostly because he found himself reluctant to tell her the truth about his feelings, thoughts, and memories. He also found himself fearing her gradually increasing dramatic emotional reactions and associations. He has been browsing on-line dating services (Match. com. is his current favorite) and is almost ready to take the plunge of listing himself. Harvey knows he tends to choose wounded partners who will co-create conflicted relationships with him, but has gotten better at discerning healthier partners and at setting good boundaries for himself and intimate friends and lovers. He and Theo have been exchanging referrals for seventeen years and trust each other's integrity and clinical skills.

Don and Nancy are on the way to their first therapy session.

It's 8:45 A.M. and Don is dressed for work in slacks and a nice blue shirt. Nancy's dressed in a peach skirt and black chemise with pearl earrings and matching necklace. She's wearing expensive perfume that Don has never told her he dislikes. She looks good and knows it. Don is driving them in his silver Mercedes, and is worried and angry. He's alternating between obsessing about Denise, reminding himself of his resolve to keep his family together, and fearing Nancy's anger and condemnations. Meanwhile Nancy is working herself into a self-righteous rage in an ongoing attempt to make all their problems about Don's infidelity:

Don: *"What a mess. But it's best to keep the family together. I won't do to my kids what my parents did to my sisters and me."* He suddenly thinks of Denise and feels a wave of loss followed by guilt. *"Here's the turn-off."*

Nancy: *"He lied so much. How could I not know? He never talks to me. Maybe this therapist can get him to talk."* "You're going to have to talk about your affair to Dr. Brown, Don. You can't lie to him."

Don: *"Not going to answer questions about how often we did it. At least twice a week and it was great. You haven't been interested in years, Nancy. I need love and you don't want it with me. Why let it bug you if I get it someplace else?"* "Look, we need to work this out, but we'll be there in five minutes. Let's not fight now."

Nancy: Staring out the window. *"We haven't had sex in months, and I haven't said anything because I can't stand the way he touches me. O God! His hands all over her. They've been doing it for a year! Is he even attracted to me now? What if the kids find out? Michael's only eleven, but he'll be all right. Julie's so unhappy, and she always blames me. What can we possibly say to them? What an asshole!"*

21

"You're such an asshole! You're a father. Julie's just fifteen. This will break her heart."

Don: *"God, I hope Julie doesn't find out. Messed up as she is. She used to be so cute. Don, you jerk! Don't do this to her. It's just like Nancy to tell her."* "There's no need for the kids to hear about this."

Nancy: *"Then why did you fuck Denise, of all people? She's been to our parties. She's met the kids."* "You've already screwed Julie up with your neglect, while you've been off fucking that whore."

Don: *"This is what she'll keep harping on. This is the whole therapy session. I'm an asshole for fucking someone else, and Denise is the whore."* "It doesn't do any good to talk like that."

Nancy: Triumphant, check mate. "Right! You never want to talk about anything."

We are always creating meaning out of who we are and what we experience.

Don and Nancy are miserable at this moment because their current life stories are generating confusion, lack of resolve, and unnecessary suffering. Both are caught up in defensive states that are intersubjectively blending into a relational defensive pattern. Don is unclear about what his work is as a man and a husband, and is internally surrendering to angry beliefs that attack Nancy while he externally tries to advocate for positive change. This cripples his ability to do what it takes to make love work. Nancy is avoiding feeling and honoring her wounded femininity and deep vulnerability by shoveling coal into the angry furnace of her outrage at Don.

We are always creating meaning out of who we are and what we experience. Different states of consciousness can involve different sets of memories, associations, and life stories. Neither Don nor Nancy currently believes that they have conscious choice in this meaning making. Defensive states influence us to resist mature, conscious, self-reflective discernment.

As they're driving to the session, Don and Nancy both believe that the meaning they're creating is the only truth possible under the circumstances. Like most people in defensive states, they are wrong. If either considered the multiple perspectives available, and consciously chose to embrace the ones that best met their beautiful, good, and true validity standards, both would have a different experience.

Don could cultivate compassion and depth of consciousness to wake up to the fact he has activated a defensive state of amplified feelings, distorted beliefs and perceptions, and destructive impulses. He could refuse to indulge this state, learn what a good man should do in this kind of situation, and resolve to do his best to be true to his principles and help Nancy be a well loved, radiant woman. If he did all these things, he might be thinking:

> *"Nancy deserves my presence and integrity, and I've let her down. I've let our sex life go to hell as much as she has. Denise was my way of collapsing away from taking a stand for love with Nancy. I need to get a hold of myself, live by my principles, and be present for her. I need to love her and open her with tenderness, understanding, and humor until she rediscovers the caring, passionate, beautiful woman that she really is."*

Similarly, Nancy could cultivate compassion and depth of consciousness so that she is aware of her defensive state. She could refuse to indulge that state and dedicate herself to being a wellspring of love—a source of radiant light—who can discern fresh current emotion from old toxic residue, and can choose to serve love in the moment. If she did all these things, she might be thinking:

> *"Of course Don's had an affair. I've denied him warmth, humor, devotional love, and erotic radiance. I've refused to insist that we learn to talk intimately and easily. No self-respecting man takes that forever. I need to feel my love for him in my heart. I need to show him my pleasure when he's his best self. I need to show him my suffering, not my contempt and rage, when he's not his best self.*

23

> *I need to nourish the feminine in me like a flower with daily pleasure in the body, and then let it shine out to Don and the kids. It's my responsibility as a woman and as his feminine partner"*

Their inability to shift their meaning making from indulging defensive states to cultivating health and love is the real reason they've entered therapy, though what each consciously believes is that the main problem is their spouse being uncaring, messed up, and needing help. It's Dr. Theo Brown's job to help them grow and expand fast enough so they can sustain hope, but not push so hard that their defenses go into overdrive and they flee from therapy, or decompensate and go crazy.

The first session.

While Don and Nancy are driving to the session, Dr. Theo Brown opens his office, puts tea water on to boil, and reviews case notes for the clients he's seeing today. *"Eight appointments; 6:00 still open. 10:00, 12:00, 1:00, and 4:00 have been doing well. 11:00, 3:00, and 5:00 can get pretty explosive, and the new couple is a wild card."* He hears the door to the waiting room open and shut, and gets up from his desk. *"Here we go."*

> Theo: Don and Nancy are sitting on the couch as Theo opens the door. There is a palpable feeling of fear and hostility in the little waiting room. *"This is going to be intense. They look healthy though. She has radiance (nice earrings and blouse), and he looks like a decent, moderately successful man."* "Welcome. Come on back and sit down. Can I get you some tea or water?" Pleasantries are exchanged as everybody gets settled into chairs:
>
> Theo: "Would you like a tape of the session to listen to at home?"
>
> Don: Alarmed. "I don't think so."
>
> Nancy: "Maybe not."
>
> Theo: Given that an affair is involved and people feel especially vulnerable around embarrassing secrets, Theo's

not surprised. He breathes deeply while slowing his pulse and releasing muscular tension, knowing that if he's in a relaxed, matter-of-fact state, it will help them feel more secure and normalize what they discuss. Both seem threatened at the moment, so his focus is to relate in ways that help them feel cared about and safe. He looks them in the eyes and smiles. "No problem. So, what brings us together?"

Nancy: With an aura of expertise. "We have communication problems. Don won't talk about anything. There are lots of issues."

Theo: *"First help her feel heard and validated. Then get Don involved. He seems to look to her to take the lead."* "OK, I can tell just by the tension in the room that there are issues, and if you could communicate productively about emotionally charged issues, you probably wouldn't be here. How about you, Don? What do you want to accomplish today?"

Don: A little stiffly. "I want to keep my family together. Nancy's been threatening divorce."

Theo: *"Here comes the affair. Let her vent about it first. She's probably been overwhelmed by the shock and doesn't know where to go with it."* "It sounds like there's been a huge recent issue, Nancy."

Nancy: "Don said he told you about the affair."

Theo: *"Relax, normalize. Help them talk about it."* "So, Don's been having an affair. How did you find out, and how have you been dealing with it?"

Nancy: Clearly feeling like the aggrieved party. "He's been with her and lying about it for a year. I saw an email and then dragged it out of him. He denied it at first. I don't know if he's still seeing her *and* she works for him."

Theo: "It must have been devastating for you. Like your world was turned upside down."

Nancy: "We have two children and what I thought was a good life. How could he do this to our family?"

25

Theo: *"Open it up, she's unsure if the affair is over. How do they talk about conflict? Let's find out."* "Don, you told me you broke it off with Denise, but Nancy says she doesn't know if you're still seeing her. Maybe you could clarify this for Nancy."

Don: Defensively. "I did break it off, Nancy, but Denise is my office manager. I have to see her every day and she does a good job."

Nancy: "A good job fucking the boss!"

Don: *"Oh no. I knew it."* "Nancy, we talked about this. I have to take care of the business. I can't just fire a key employee."

Nancy: *"I hate him seeing her every day."* "It wasn't taking care of the business to cheat on your wife. You should tell her to get the hell out and never come back. If you..."

Theo: Interrupting. It's often necessary to interrupt in couples work. The defensive states accelerate faster than in individual sessions. *"Quick acceleration to mutual attacks. Soothe her by confronting him. They're in more danger than they know."* "Nancy's right that Denise should leave the office. It complicates ending a love affair to stay in regular proximity to the person you're leaving, but you have to be enormously careful in these situations. If you asked her to leave because of your relationship, she might feel hurt and angry enough to file a sexual harassment suit. I'm not a lawyer but, since you're the boss, I think you might be vulnerable there."

Don: Appalled at the idea of this happening. It has never occurred to him that sweet Denise might attack him in this way. Theo knows that the capacity for emotional violence co-varies with the extent people create and allow negative relational drama, and so he's cautioning both of them that impulsive action right now might have big consequences, and is beginning to prepare them for unexpected drama that might be coming. This is threatening material that both Don's and Nancy's defenses resist awareness of. Don unconsciously goes to a familiar defensive position of blaming Nancy for their problems, while passive-aggressively attacking her with a reference to his lover. "Denise would never do anything like that unless Nancy went off half cocked." Looking at her. "You know you blow up and do things."

Nancy: Despairingly. "This is never going to work."

Theo: *"Enough enactment; I see their current defenses. Time to shift into more caring perspectives. They need to focus on why they're here."* "Nancy, what if this therapy worked exactly how you wanted it? What would be different?"

Nancy: Confused, as people often are when directed to confront their defenses. The power of defenses is in remaining unconscious. When defenses are exposed to the light of conscious attention, people can bring healthy discernment to bear on them, disidentify from them, and begin to soothe amplified emotion, correct distorted beliefs and perceptions, and resist destructive impulses, while feeling more empathy and self-reflective awareness. Therapy encourages clients to bring defensive states into conscious awareness, and to take on the responsibility to manage them for the highest good. Nancy's confusion is a road sign for Theo that directs him towards these productive areas. Her defenses will tend to generate confusion to resist awareness of positive aspects of her marriage, positive intent in herself and Don, and possible positive outcomes of therapy—all of which pressure her to open to new perspectives. "I don't really know. We'd communicate better and not fight so much. Don wouldn't cheat on me."

Theo: Smiling. Inspiring. "Those are pretty modest goals for optimal outcomes. How about feeling in love with each other, trusting each other, being romantically fulfilled with each other, and helping each other grow into wiser and more beautiful people?"

Don: Feeling a surge of unexpected longing. *"If only we could."* "That sounds good."

Theo: "Is that what you want, Don?"

Don: "Yes, but I don't know if it's possible."

Nancy: Somewhat surprised and touched at the vulnerability in Don's voice. "I'd love those things too, but it's been so long since we've felt anything like them."

Theo: Providing an interpretation. "Think about when you first met. I'll bet you liked each other, were attracted, grew to love each other and became romantically and erotically involved. Your individual defenses have gathered momentum over the years and you've gradually developed negative patterns of relating. Now you need to change those patterns to get back to love. Anger blocks love. Distrust blocks love. Closure blocks love. If you can work to resolve your anger, trust each other, and open to each other instead of close down, you have a good chance of consistently feeling love again."

Nancy: "That sounds great, but how do we do it?"

Theo: "First, learn how to discern between healthy expression and emotional violence. A good beginning is to have zero tolerance for insulting each other or putting each other down."

In the above session, Theo is cultivating compassion and depth of consciousness in himself and Don and Nancy to improve the central relationships in their conflicts. These include, but are not limited to, Nancy and Don's relationships with their individual defenses, with different aspects of each other, with their marriage and family as entities, with each of their children, with Theo, with Don's business, with Denise, and with their individual and collective futures.

Don's and Nancy's defenses, in unconscious efforts to avoid change, push them to make these relationships dark, confusing, unresolved, conflicted, and hopeless, generating impulses to do emotional violence to themselves and others. Theo is encouraging them to begin to shift their perspectives to become healthier in all their inner and interpersonal relationships. The way he does this is by using his own relationships with himself and them to:

- **Relate**: Relating involves Theo attuning to himself and them. Attuning to himself is cultivating awareness of his own sensations, emotions, thoughts, and impulses with acceptance and caring intent. Such self-attunement is essential to therapeutic relationships because, in the constantly shifting intersubjective currents of the session, Theo's sensations, feelings, thoughts, and impulses all inform him how everyone is doing and what might help. As he attunes to himself, he can extend his awareness to attune to each of them, subjectively feeling into what they might be feeling, thinking, and wanting with acceptance and caring intent. Attunement is a central feature of most psychotherapeutic systems.[1]

- **Teach**: Theo is alert for opportunities to present them with techniques, information, and perspectives that reflect more compassion and deeper consciousness than the ones they have, as when Theo suggests that they begin moving back towards love by cultivating zero tolerance for insulting each other or putting each other down.

- **Inspire**: Most people become inspired to consider new ways of thinking and being when presented with visions of—or momentary peak experiences of—superior functioning that they have real possibilities of attaining (as when Theo suggests goals of love and passion). Such perspectives and experiences model superior, constructive relating rather than destructive defensive ways of dealing with issues (one example of this is when Theo talks about the affair without pathologizing or blaming).

- **Confront**: Confrontation is simply articulating healing truths that challenge others to shift perspectives, as when Theo confronts Don that Nancy is probably right about Denise needing to leave the business.

- **Interpret**: There are endless perspectives available to us at any time. Healing interpretation is when a therapist offers new perspectives that uncover unconscious material and support more compassionate understanding and creative healing action. Theo provides such an interpretation when he suggests that their original love for each other was being masked by defensive habits of closure that they both had unconsciously allowed to gain momentum over the years.

29

This supports each changing their personal narrative toward being more positive, coherent, and optimistic about their chances of growing and improving their relationships. It also teaches them that they can positively change their life story by cultivating healing perspectives.

- **Direct**: Every client I've ever worked with has wanted to know what I believed served the highest good for them and others. Healthy direction includes encouraging (but rarely demanding) specific perspectives and actions that the therapist believes are necessary and/or preferable, as when Theo suggests that Don be enormously careful about how he eases Denise out of his business.

Theo's goals, or organizing principles, as he engages in the session are to ease (or remediate) their symptoms, enhance their health, and support their development by using his relationships with himself and them to help improve Don and Nancy's own intrapersonal and interpersonal relationships. These improvements will manifest as integrations towards deeper, more compassionate understanding, more capacities to stop closing and more effectively open moments, and wider embrace of self and others towards unity.

Endnotes

[1] Witt (2007)

CHAPTER THREE

Who Relates?

"I was so much older then, I'm younger than that now."
~Bob Dylan~

Here are Don and Nancy at The Coffee Cat on Anacapa Street in Santa Barbara after their session. Each has scheduled an individual session with Theo (Don for 6:00 PM that night and Nancy in two days), and they've been directed to do their best to use kind tones, avoid insulting or hostile references, and not talk about the affair unless they are in session with Theo. Both are trying to observe these suggestions and as a result are stiff and practically immobilized. Theo predicted this might happen and told them new habits often feel awkward and can take months to institute and maybe years of practice to become natural reactions:

Don: Feeling more positively connected to Nancy than he has in months. *"She looks good in that blouse. Theo said I should compliment her more."* "You look good in that blouse."

Nancy: Pleasantly surprised but guarded. She has a vague sense of loss around being discouraged from indulging self-righteous moral outrage, but likes the feeling of connection with Don. "Thanks. I thought the session went well."

Don: Also guarded. He's conditioned to avoid most forms of intimate talk because it usually devolves into him lying by omission or commission, and Nancy attacking him with insults or hostile analysis. On the other hand, Theo told him to be honest and transparent with Nancy. "I think I finally have hope for us."

Nancy: Feeling a flood of rage. *"He finally has hope? What's he done to create hope? Fuck his office manager? Lie to me?"* "What do you mean 'finally'? Why have you stayed

> if you've thought it's hopeless? Because I take care of
> your life; that's why. I'm not your wife; I'm your mommy.
> You've never worked through your family stuff, and you
> cheated on me just like your father cheated on your
> mother."

> Don: *"Here we go. To hell with her. This will never work. I
> wonder if Denise will come into the office today."* "I've got
> to go."

Who are these people? Are they the awkward, more caring individuals in the first exchange, consciously trying to do right and serve love? Are they the defensive, egocentric, and less caring individuals that are collapsing into the smooth grooves of their defensive impulses (Denise to cling and torture, and Don to demean and withdraw) in the second exchange? Or are they some mix of these and other aspects?

The answer, of course, is that they are all of the above and more. Who we are in a given instant varies depending upon our state of consciousness, our level of development in a variety of areas, the type of person we are (especially masculine or feminine type), and our immediate environmental cues.

The self-line of development, characterological and neurotic defenses.

As we briefly explored in Chapter One, our current self is a combination of the "I" whom we subjectively sense we always have been, and the "I" that is always changing, shifting, expanding, and contracting. We are conceived as biochemical events, born into a universe of pure sensation, and then proceed to grow in intimate relationship with multiple aspects of others and ourselves through predictable developmental stages as unique individuals. We all grow through the same stages (or levels), we don't skip stages, and *we never lose our capacity to inhabit any stage we've been.*[1]

Human growth is dominated by developmental imperatives that have their roots in the creation of life a billion years ago. Don and Nancy were both born in the grip of various developmental drives that constantly propel and inform them. These include the drives to survive, to create meaning[2], to relate to others[3], to be true to deepest masculine or feminine sexual essence[4], and to inhabit positions on personally important social hierarchies (like family, friends, school, and work)[5]. Each human's developing body, mind, spirit, and social networks are directed and influenced by such drives from birth to death.

Within two hours after birth, Don and Nancy could distinguish (and prefer) their parents' faces from other caregivers. By around seven months of age Don and Nancy had discovered that their physical bodies were separate from the world around them. In terms of self-awareness, this could be considered the birth of their physical selves.[6] At twelve months they could walk, experience shame at social disapproval, and be aware of the need for external support to regulate painful emotion.[7] Gradually as they matured to eighteen months and their brains developed the capacities for explicit memories,[8] they grew to have internalized images and beginning vocalizations that led to internalized symbols, beginning concepts, and language.[9]

At around fifteen months they began encountering the painful discovery that they were emotionally separate from their parents (especially their mothers). In terms of self-awareness this could be considered the birth of their emotional selves. If we don't successfully negotiate our individuation into separate emotional selves we run the risk of developing characterological defense structures that can vary in intensity from being an occasional absorbing negative state under huge stress, to being a stable self-destructive trait in the most supportive and benign circumstances.

Under perceived threat characterological defensive structures can manifest as characterological defensive states where we have huge difficulties distinguishing emotionally between self and others. This can lead to us treating others as objects to defensively attack, desert, or avoid with little or no insight into any damage we might inflict. When Nancy was angry enough with Don she tried to extinguish the immature raging fires in her body by attacking the parts of Don that threatened her, having no insight into how repulsive and destructive her behavior was. When Don was threatened enough by Nancy he tried to avoid the immature collapsing part of himself by demeaning and then deserting her (immaturely collapsing) with practically no awareness of the damage this caused him and her.

Between two and six, as their language skills flourished, Don and Nancy's abilities to manipulate concepts blossomed. As they developed enhanced abilities to manipulate concepts they began to *unconsciously* use those skills to fulfill the developmental demands of their drives to survive, create meaning, relate, be true to their sexual essences, and occupy positions on personally important social hierarchies, as well as to reduce or avoid anxiety, shame, or other painful emotions and/or thoughts. Unconsciously manipulating concepts means that they could repress, alter, or change concepts that felt threatening to them.

This, combined with the ongoing internal and external processes of disapproval evoking shame emotions and the accompanying drive to reduce, avoid, or get others to regulate shame emotions[10], contributed to the inevitable development of neurotic defensive tendencies. Here is where the classic defense mechanisms of repression, dissociation, suppression, projection, sublimation, reaction formation, scapegoating, and all the other neurotic internal manipulations are reflexively and unconsciously mobilized to avoid distressing truths.

The difference between neurotic defenses and characterological defenses is that, when neurotic defensive states are evoked, we have relatively more ability to soothe amplified emotion, self-reflect on our destructive impulses and distorted perspectives, and have some empathy for those who threaten us.

When Nancy caught her impulse to be nasty to Julie about the dirty bathroom and apologized, she was having insight into her neurotic defensive state and self-regulated toward love. When Don had the impulse to avoid calling Theo for a session, but instead forced himself to make the call, he was doing the same.

Neurotic defenses are much more common (and, usually, less dangerous) than characterological defenses. Both involve internal lies, and much of therapy is uncovering internal lies and evaluating them with our beautiful, good, and true validity standards so that new, healthier, more honest perspectives can be perceived and embraced.

In all the sessions in this book each individual (including therapists) oscillates between healthy responses to the present moment and defensive states. It is the therapist's job to stay attuned to self and client to monitor and work with these oscillations to improve intrapersonal and interpersonal relationships. As these relationships improve, the foundation goals of therapy (remediating symptoms, enhancing health, and supporting development) are gradually accomplished.

Healthy responses to the present moment are an individual's best, most caring response to the current environment given their resources and level of maturity. At the Coffee Cat, Don and Nancy's first exchange, although awkward and short lived, reflected healthy responses to the present moment. They were trying to do right and be caring people with what they had available to give.

I've been frequently inspired observing people doing their best to be caring and do right, especially when they are gripped in defensive states that demand emotional violence. It is on these battlefields that we can both suffer some of our worst suffering and achieve some of our most transformative and transcendent moments of love and insight.

Don's first individual session.

Theo scheduled individual sessions with Don and Nancy—with the condition that both sign releases so that Theo wouldn't be bound to keep secrets—for several reasons. People often reveal aspects of themselves in individual sessions that don't show up in conjoint sessions, and can reveal perspectives, beliefs, and behaviors that they conceal, sometimes unconsciously, from their spouses and themselves.

As the following session progresses, you can observe how Don and Theo shift frequently from one state of consciousness to another. This is a constant feature of human existence. Different perspectives, conditions, relationships, and activities either evoke or demand different states of consciousness. Giving a lecture, listening to a lecture, meditating, or playing with our three-year-old daughter all involve different states of consciousness; states evoked by the combination of who we are and what we're experiencing.

Our natural tendencies to learn and grow are compromised by our self-protective reflexes to enter defensive states when we feel threatened. Healthy development involves becoming increasingly conscious of our states of healthy response and defensive states, and being gradually more able to self-regulate into states of healthy response when we enter defensive states. Throughout life, this growth current is characterized by progressively disidentifying with defensive states, and identifying more with healthy states characterized by increasing compassion and depth of consciousness.

Don arrives five minutes early for his 6:00 P.M. session, and a spectacular sunset dominates the sky through the waiting room window. Theo opens the door with a tired expression on his face. This is his ninth session of the day and he's looking forward to dinner with his family in ninety minutes, but he is also glad to see Don. Theo feels attuned to Don and Nancy and has a general sense of direction as to what Don's next steps probably need to be. Don has had a tough day enduring Nancy's coldness during and after the argument at the Coffee Cat, followed by Denise's distracting presence at work. As Don discussing how he and Denise agreed she should find another job, Theo observes his sense of loss:

Theo: *"It's beginning to sink in that he's really losing her. He's grieving."* "I imagine it's hard for you to split up with Denise."

Don: "You have no idea."

Theo: Remembering how, at twenty-two, he lost ten pounds and cried daily for two weeks after his first lover left him, Theo leans in. *"What he's feeling must be more intense that what I felt after Mary left me."* "Tell me. Help me understand."

Don: "I love her. The only reason I'm staying with Nancy is the kids."

Theo: He perceives Don would rather talk about the problems of staying with Nancy than his grief over losing Denise. Knowing that Don needs clarity and a strong sense of mission to effectively handle his breakup with Denise, Theo stays focused on clarifying what Don's purpose is in his relationship with Denise. Masculine people do best when they know their purpose in the moment and are fully committed to it. *"Is Don really separating from Denise, or is he trying to keep her in the wings until he has made an honorable, but unsuccessful, attempt to reconcile with his wife?"* "How did your relationship with Denise develop?"

Don: Relaxing somewhat. "I hired her two years ago and we were just instantly friends. She's a great office manager and has been a huge plus. I don't know how I can replace her."

Theo: Momentarily distracted by the possible double meaning of "replace her." *"Focus, we'll get to it."* "But somehow you transitioned into becoming lovers."

Don: Talking naturally now. "Becoming lovers" is much more palatable, and reflective of his subjective experience, than "cheating on your wife." "We had some business lunches, and it was easy to talk to her. Also, she is so beautiful. After awhile, I just kissed her one day, and, wow, electricity. It went on from there. She's been wonderful, though it's been hard for her that I'm married."

Theo: *"She must be suffering a lot right now."* "I'm assuming it's hard on both of you to split up. I hope she's seeing a therapist."

Don: "She said she made an appointment with one of the people you put on the list for her. I really miss her."

Theo: "I imagine you're grieving a lot now. It's got to be hard to have her in the office."

Don: "She's looking for another job. She suggested it, not me."

Theo: "Good for her. It sounds like she's trying to do right."

Don: "She's a sweet person." His eyes fill up with tears.

Theo: Gently, feeling Don's need for validation of his loss. "You miss her."

Don: Crying now. "I could talk to her about anything. She was always so supportive. Not like Nancy." His voice hardens with anger, and his tears stop.

Theo: *"He needs to choose to love Nancy; he can't stay just for the kids."* "Then why are you leaving Denise?"

Don: Self-righteously. "For my kids. I can't put them through a divorce."

Theo: "Is that the only reason? You sound as if love is not possible with Nancy."

Don: "We were great in the beginning. We had great sex, we laughed and had fun. I don't know what happened to her. It seems that as soon as we started trying to have kids she got hard and bossy. Now she has nothing good to say about me. She's a great mom though."

Theo: Teaching. "I believe that part of being a good parent is modeling good relationships for your kids. The best thing you and Nancy can do for them is to find a way back to love."

Don: *"Love with Nancy? She hates me."* "She hates me."

Theo: Confronting and teaching. "Of course she's pissed off. Women are programmed to have discriminative jealousy. In hunter/gatherer societies, a woman who interfered with her man falling in love with another woman had a reproductive advantage.[11] What Nancy needs to learn is how to open up her feminine erotic radiance when you're being your best self."

Don: Threatened by this new perspective of Nancy as erotically radiant, yearning to be claimed by him, Don enters a defensive state of self-doubt, depressed perspectives, and passive aggressive impulses. He laughs ruefully. "Are you kidding? The last thing in the world she wants is to be romantic with me. She says I'm disgusting."

Theo: He feels a satisfied sense of compassionate affection in his chest, which he's learned indicates attunement with his clients. He focuses on opening up from his heart area, and laughs a little. *"Confront and inspire."* "You're wrong about that, Don. Look at the books she reads. Look at how beautiful she is, and how much she takes care of her physical health. She yearns to be loved by a present, trustable man. You haven't been present or trustable. When she got distracted by being a mother and conflicted about sex, you deserted her."

Don: He enters a neurotic defensive state where he's threatened at the challenge, feels unjustly accused, clings to the belief that he has done everything he could or should, and surrenders to the impulse to argue with Theo, not noticing the irony of arguing with the man he's hired to give him expert opinions. "I paid the bills. I gave her space. I never cheated on her the first seventeen years of our marriage."

Theo: *"Help him understand her."* "A feminine person suffers if love is not happening. You are unsafe to Nancy because it looks to her like that's OK with you."

Don: Defensively, sounding like a five-year-old. "You sound like Nancy. It's all my fault."

Theo: Feeling affection and admiration. This is a good man. *"Challenge him to be a superior man."* "One of the best relationship teachers I've had, David Deida, says there are three kinds of relationships: first stage, second stage, and third stage.

First stage relationships are egocentric. Women are radiant to get attention and resources, while men use their presence to get validation and sex for themselves. Neither is particularly caring of others. I know you and Denise have felt deep love for each other, but your relationship has been destructive to your life, family, and business, and Denise's life, job, and prospects for healthy intimacy. It is mostly a first stage, egocentric relationship where you both are pursuing pleasures and gratification at the price of suffering for lots of people, including yourselves.

Second stage relationships are egalitarian, fifty/fifty, and based on fairness and negotiation. You have your space, and I have mine. That's where you and Nancy have been for years. Passion often fades in second stage relationships because men are afraid to assert their purpose, focus, and shadow, and women are afraid to inhabit their feminine radiance.

Third stage relationships are all about giving your best gifts to the world and opening your partner to pleasure, growth, passion, and meaning. As a masculine partner, your job is to anchor in your principles, purpose, humor, and shadow, and offer her your best love and direction and stand unrecoiling at whatever her response. Most of us have first stage, second stage, and third stage moments every day. The more we grow, the more third stage moments we have until we either die, or the third stage becomes our main mode of relating. Deida has written a great book about this called *The Way of the Superior Man[12].*"

Don: Intrigued, doubtful, but in a state of healthy response to the present moment. "What if I do that and Nancy still hates me?"

Theo: *"Here we go into forbidden territory."* "If you consistently offer your best gifts and deepest consciousness to her, and she can't learn to receive you with pleasure, then the healthy thing to do is to leave her."

Don: Astounded that a Psychologist is telling him he might have to leave his wife. This does not meet his "good" validity standard. It feels immoral to him as an option. "Isn't it wrong to divorce?"

Theo: Teaching. "Our ethical standards, our principles, don't change as we mature as much as they become refined. Of course it's usually better for everyone if a husband and wife can find their way back to love. But, if one person grows enough to give their best gifts and the other can't or won't grow enough to receive those gifts with pleasure, then all you can do is leave, give your partner a chance to find love someplace else, and model for your children how to live by your principles and choose love. Nancy is suffering from not having enough love in her life. What if she became erotically radiant, emotionally generous, and self-soothing when she was angry, and you kept ignoring her or cheating on her? Shouldn't she leave under those circumstances?"

Don: Getting it, like masculine people often do, in a rush and then making an internal commitment from his core of integrity. "Of course, but I don't think she can do those things."

Theo: *"I think she can."* "Don't sell her short, but that's not your job to be responsible for her growth. Your responsibility is to learn how to be a present, trustable, unrecoiling man who knows her heart and claims her each day with love."

Don: Feeling inspired. "I'd like to be that man."

Theo: "It's my job to help you."

In this session, Don's first stage (egocentric) self, second stage (everything has to be fair) self, and third stage (serve the highest good) self all made appearances. He moved in and out of defensive states and states of healthy response to the present moment. All this was guided by his executive ego, his observing self, generally staying focused on his purpose in the session, to do what was best for his family. Don's observing ego was constantly relating to Theo, and to the various aspects of himself that were evoked as he discussed his relationships with Nancy, Denise, his kids, and others. As this was happening Don's *subjective* sense of self stayed the same, even though his worldviews, states of consciousness, opinions, and even memory sets varied dramatically.

Theo, similarly, was moving in and out of various states of consciousness, relating to all his reactions. He was using his physical, emotional, spiritual, and relational selves as instruments to inform and guide him as he related to Don and everyone Don was affiliated with including Nancy, the kids, and Denise. Unlike Don, Theo was aware of how his and Don's perspectives shifted with morphing states of consciousness, and was deliberately cultivating states of increased compassion and self-reflective insight in them both.

We are all complex communities of interrelating parts (many at different levels of development) guided by our consciousness and driven by a multitude of internal and external forces. In a way we are colony organisms of clustered relationships moving in different directions depending upon myriad conscious, unconscious, relational, and environmental factors. My colony organism of clustered relationships encounters your colony organism of clustered relationships, and intersubjective energy fields automatically constellate and influence both of us, attracting or repelling, opening or closing. These energetic polarities will vary, often predictably, depending upon many factors including whether our deepest essences are more masculine or more feminine, whether we are in defensive states or states of healthy response, and what levels we currently are operating at on various developmental lines.

Endnotes

[1] Wilber (2000)
[2] Kegan (1982)
[3] Siegel (1999)
[4] Deida (2004)
[5] Adler (1956)
[6] Wilber (2000)
[7] Schore (2003)
[8] Seigel (1999)
[9] Wilber (2000)
[10] Witt (2007)
[11] Deida (2004)
[12] Deida (1997)

CHAPTER FOUR

Polarity

I love the way you do me babe
I love the way you pump
I love the way you do me babe
Humph, humph, arumph

I've seen your act a thousand times
Baby you crunch and crumph
And every time you knock me out
Humph, humph, arumph

Love you fingers grinding on my hips
Love that smile shining on your lips
Oh baby, that last kiss…
Humph, humph, arupmh

~from *Humph Humph Arumph*~

Here are Don and Nancy the night of his individual session. He was distracted all the way home reliving moments of the session and having accompanying flashes of feelings, memories, and thoughts. Don is eating lasagna at the kitchen table while Nancy's having a cup of tea. The kids are in their rooms, and they can hear Marylyn Manson thudding through Julie's door. Nancy rolls her eyes, and they look at each other and smile somewhat guardedly:

Nancy: "I hate that music. How was your session?"

Don: *"This is nice."* "It was good."

Nancy: Like most feminine people Nancy is emotionally and energetically sensitive, and so she can feel Don holding back when she's connected with him. The familiar withholding hurts, but this is a pleasant scene and, remembering the direction from their conjoint session, she tries to use a warm tone. "What was good?"

Don: Unconsciously relaxing in response to her friendly voice. *"What did Theo say I should tell her?"* "We talked about what I could do to help you and me love each other better."

Nancy: She is unexpectedly moved, and literally stops breathing for a second. *"How sweet."* "That's so sweet."

Don: Feeling suddenly tender towards her. "I want us to be happy together."

This is a moment of erotic polarity between Don and Nancy. He presents her with presence, with intention to do right, and has been well coached in how to express the most compassionate truth about his session. Nancy receives his effort and feels pleasure in her body, and trusts him enough to let the pleasure show in ways he can sense and enjoy.

Polarity is everywhere.

There are energetic components to every relationship we have with others and ourselves.[1] We look at a mountain and feel something. You and I exchange a glance and we both feel something. I shift in my chair to ease a pain in my back and I feel something. You remember an embarrassing episode from your past and you feel something. These thoughts, feelings, and accompanying impulses are indicators of energetic polarities that characterize the relationships between me and the mountain, you and me, me and the pain in my back, and you and your embarrassing episode.

Energetic polarities can be healthy or unhealthy, constructive or destructive. A fistfight, a screaming argument, or staying up late worrying about problems all involve lots of energetic polarities. Obsessive thought is an out-of-control polarity between me and whatever I am obsessing about. Meditation, centering prayer, interested observation, and passionate caress also involve energetic polarities. Compassionate regard creates loving polarity between us and the object of our attention.

To the extent we are conscious of these energies, and disciplined in how we focus our attention, we can influence polarities. This illustrates how, psychologically and spiritually, energy follows thought.[2]

Erotic polarity, a powerful force in adult bonding, vulnerable to defenses.

Erotic polarity often occurs when a masculine energy source and a feminine energy source encounter each other. Feminine erotic radiance pulls and amplifies masculine attention. Trustable masculine presence evokes and amplifies feminine erotic radiance. Destructive or toxic energies such as critical attack or passive aggressive withdrawal block and diminish positive erotic polarity.

Don and Nancy's erotic polarity has been dulled in a variety of ways. Some of these diminishments were unavoidable consequences of a couple passing from romantic infatuation into more intimate family bonding.[3] Other diminishments were functions of Don and Nancy not embracing their responsibilities as masculine and feminine partners in a lover relationship.

Romantic infatuation and intimate bonding.

Most marital relationships begin with romantic infatuation, driven by the neurochemicals norepinephrine and dopamine (which are involved in excitement, or arousal, of many kinds). As couples become more intimate, their closeness begins to approximate the levels of connection that they experienced in their families of origin. Deepening intimacy and family of origin associations cause the relationship to progress to a bonding stage where the couple's emotional connection is additionally mediated by the attachment neurotransmitters of vasopressin in men and oxytocin in women.[4] This stage of relational attachment often requires more conscious effort to maintain erotic polarity.

I suspect this is due partly to the incest taboos that are present in all cultures and families. As attachment approximates family of origin levels, automatic blocks to sexual polarity, arousal, and conscious awareness of sexual needs and feelings can kick in, probably at least partly because these experiences were taboo between family members.

Additionally, there genetic imperatives in men to be attracted to and erotically claim desirable women, and in women to yearn for—and erotically bond with—powerful and/or trustable men. Without the power of romantic infatuation keeping lovers literally intoxicated with each other, these drives can influence us toward constellating romantic infatuation with others.

In the absence of conscious effort, erotic polarity can fade, often contributing to the kinds of suffering that Don and Nancy are confronting. Further, the demands of family responsibilities, work, and aging all tend to diminish our energy levels in general and our sense of ourselves as erotic beings in particular. Once again, in the absence of conscious effort to counter these influences, erotic polarity can fade.

Defenses and polarity.

If people are unaware of the above processes, defensive structures and states can be cued by the diminishment of polarity and the increase of subjective stress. People feel less attractive as they feel less attracted to their spouses, and the anxiety and distress of this can stir up reflexive defenses against threat and emotional pain. If we learned to be self-critical as a defense against perceived threat, we will have tendencies to attack ourselves under stress. If we learned to blame others as a defense, we will have tendencies to attack others (often family members). The fear, anger, and emotional violence of these defenses can diminish erotic polarity, just as fear, anger, and emotional violence tend to diminish warm, loving, affectionate feelings of all sorts.

When Don and Nancy first met, they had major erotic polarity. Sex was frequent, and each felt driven to caress, possess, and be possessed by the other. Caught up in the romantic infatuation stage of relationship, and unaware that they were choosing each other for their complementary wounds as well as complementary dreams, they had no idea that easy sexual polarity could eventually fade and require conscious attention. They were unprepared for the emotional violence that would emerge from their defensive structures/states and deepening family of origin associations. They had no conceptual context to provide understanding or direction when romantic infatuation waned and defensive states were more urgently evoked.

When erotic polarity is hot, couples can easily forgive individual differences and defensive states. Erotic polarity can be a biochemical vacation from our defenses (though jealousy is a notable exception). When erotic polarity is allowed to diminish without healing adjustment, it causes suffering to the partners and threatens secure attachment. This suffering and threat can evoke relational defensive patterns. Relational defenses can amplify until there is a breakdown of some sort, just as a water heater explodes when the thermostat is broken and the pressure keeps building. Don's affair with Denise was just such an explosion.

Part of Theo's job is to convey all this information to Don and Nancy in ways that are understandable to their particular worldviews, and non-threatening enough to maintain the therapy session as a safe environment. As he does this he will frequently engage their defensive states. Among these dozens of intrapersonal and interpersonal relationships, a guiding principle for Theo is to keep focused on perceiving and supporting the erotic polarity that is at the heart of Don and Nancy's love affair. Even though they are largely unaware of its power, this love affair is what can distinguish their relationship from all others. Renewing and supporting it is an essential aspect of healing the attachment wounds they have created in their marriage. Consciously cultivating a shared practice of enhancing love supports development, makes repair of emotional injuries more possible, and enhances progressive integration individually and interpersonally.

Nancy's first individual session.

Ten AM on Thursday morning, Nancy walks into Theo's waiting room for an individual session. She's wearing a tight peach top, faded blue jeans, sandals, and sparkly earrings. Theo opens the door to a feminine rush of Gardenia perfume and Nancy's friendly smile:

Theo: He feels the pleasant warmth of her femininity. *"Nice, attractive. This is how she probably is normally with people. I need to help her offer this to Don when he's present and attentive."* He smiles, using his masculine presence to shape the erotic polarity that has been constellated in the room to help her further relax and open. "It's good to see you. Come on back." He gets her a cup of tea and they get settled.

Theo: What were your reactions to our last session?"

Nancy: "I thought Don opened up more than usual."

Theo: *"What about you, Nancy?"* "Do you have any questions?"

Nancy: Comfortable talking about Don, she unconsciously pathologizes him and tries to make all their problems about the affair. "Is he still seeing her? You saw him Tuesday night."

Theo: Supporting the concept of Don's integrity being sacred and attractive. "It looks to me like Don's telling the truth and trying to do right by everybody. I believe he told Denise that they can't see each other, and that he's going to work on improving his marriage with you."

Nancy: *"It's so embarrassing he cheated."* "He's been lying for so long it's hard to believe him."

Theo: *"Make it about her."* "How has it been for you this last year?"

Nancy: Confused as her resistance to discussing herself is subtly challenged. "What do you mean?"

Theo: "Have you felt more loving or less loving with Don and the kids? Have you felt more satisfied or less satisfied with your life? How has it been to be you this last year?"

Nancy: Uncomfortable and feeling defensive. "Everything seemed pretty much normal. We're very busy people."

Theo: Pressing her to be more personal as he feels compassion and an interior sense of moving into fruitful territory. "How satisfying has your marriage been?"

Nancy: Strangely reluctant to talk. *"Satisfying? What is he talking about?"* "I've been busy with the kids, and with running our lives."

Theo: "What happened to your and Don's romantic relationship?"

Nancy: Now very uncomfortable. Unconsciously going to her defensive touchstone when dealing with marital dissatisfaction, blaming Don. "He's always working or playing tennis, and we're so tired every night. He'll want to have sex and we haven't said a word to each other all day."

Theo: "So you find his overtures repulsive?"

Nancy: *"Yes, but that sounds gross to be repulsed."* "He just always asks at a bad time."

Theo: *"She's lost touch with her yearning."* "I imagine it's been quite a loss for you. You and Don were pretty hot and heavy in the beginning."

Nancy: Smiles and lights up a little, remembering the morning after they became engaged when she and Don blew off work to make love all morning. She tells Theo the story she's learned to tell herself. "Everybody's hot in the beginning and then life takes over."

Theo: Recognizing that Nancy has become disconnected from her erotically radiant feminine core. *"Be delicate. Reach her feminine radiance through her conceptual self; she's more comfortable thinking, it's less threatening."* "When people first meet they are drawn to each other's wounds and dreams. They fall into romantic infatuation, which is mediated by brain systems dominated by dopamine and norepinephrine, excitement neurotransmitters. Romantic infatuation is a biochemical vacation from many defenses. As you become bonded, you activate systems run by oxytocin, a bonding neurotransmitter. Intimate bonding means you approximate the depth of connection you had growing up with family members, which, under stress, cues the defenses you developed as a child. When such defenses kick in, the real work of intimacy begins. For you it became much more difficult to inhabit erotic radiance, and be the sex goddess."

Nancy: The words, "sex Goddess" feel both pleasurable and vaguely transgressive. She unconsciously retreats to attacking Don. "I've done my part. It's Don that couldn't hold up his end."

Theo: Gently confronting. "Have you arranged to be erotically radiant, a wellspring of love for Don? Have you nourished your feminine self with daily bodily pleasure? Have you embraced your responsibility to establish and maintain erotic polarity with your man?"

Nancy: Confused, but liking the sound of being erotically radiant and a wellspring of love. It feels good to hear pleasure and her natural feminine eroticism acknowledged. Her resistance becomes somewhat more tentative. "There's always too much to do."

Theo: Teaching. *"Connect her with pleasure in the body."* "You're the feminine pole of the masculine/feminine erotic polarity in your and Don's relationship. Look how you feel pleasure in your body, and smile just talking about it. One of the reasons you two have so little shared eroticism is that he's learned to avoid opening you with his attention and you've learned to avoid showing him your feminine radiance and pleasure. That's the most powerful attractor in the world to a masculine person."

Nancy: Angry now. "What, I should just put out and he won't cheat on me?"

Theo: Meeting her anger with compassionate presence and depth of understanding of how she's suffered not opening and inhabiting her intensely feminine essence. Feeling through her anger to her heart. *"This is where Don deserts her."* "You've suffered not feeling erotically radiant. You've suffered not experiencing love being served in your family. You need to cultivate your feminine heart to be true to your deepest essence and to evoke his best self."

50

Nancy: Feels a pang of loss in her chest. *"I've so missed being in love."* "How can I get past the affair? It's all I can think about."

Theo: Feeling caring and drawn towards her. *"This is her feminine power; her yearning is so much more attractive than her rage."* "The way to get through this trauma is to be stronger, wiser, more radiant, and more deeply attracted to, and more in love with, Don as a result of how you deal with it. This doesn't make trauma a preferable method of growth, but it eventually makes the trauma acceptable, especially if Don does his work also."

Nancy: Confused. She has reflexively avoided thinking of Don as a desirable lover for years. *"He's never attractive, except he was sweet last night."* "When he's attentive and thoughtful he can be sweet. When he's relaxed and has a sense of humor he can be really funny."

Theo: "What do you do that evokes these parts of him?"

Nancy: "I shouldn't have to do anything."

Theo: Laughing. Feeling attuned and willing to press a little. "I completely agree. Don should be present, congruent, true to his principles, and dedicated to opening you to love and pleasure every moment he's with you, no matter how distracted or hostile you are. He might learn how to do this, but he doesn't do it consistently now. He collapses in the face of your anger and contempt. Now your relationship is run largely by habits of closure, defensive patterns. A problem you have with him is that you don't stay connected to his heart and feel the pleasure of him being his best self. Your pleasure at him being his best self is a powerful reinforcer."

Nancy Indignant. "That's just being a whore, to be all nice and sexy so he'll like me."

Theo: Responding to her 50/50 egalitarian language. This is often a signature perspective of the second stage, people denying their sexual selves and believing fairness and good communication is all it takes to make good relationships. "Is Don being a whore if he's angry or defensive, but focuses on serving you open into love and pleasure instead of surrendering to hostile impulses to attack or desert you? You want him to cultivate the traits that most please you. What traits could you cultivate to open him to be his best self?"

Nancy: "He never listens to what I say. I've been telling him for years he should get into therapy, work through his mother crap, and be a man. He just blows me off."

Theo: "You've been challenging him from your masculine side to his masculine side. Men challenge each other in these ways and happily slug it out in competitive debate. You may be accurate, but activating your masculine side kills your erotic polarity with Don. You attract your reciprocal. If you want masculine presence, generate feminine radiance."

Nancy: Suddenly having an image of Denise in the sexy red dress she wore to Don's office party. Feeling bitter. "That's what that whore does."

Theo: *"Almost there."* "You're avoiding your issues by calling Denise a whore. I agree that she's using her feminine erotic radiance for egocentric purposes. She and Don had a first stage relationship where they went for personal gratification at the cost of suffering for lots of people. You and Don have second stage, egalitarian relationship of 50/50 negotiation that minimizes the importance of him being true to his deepest masculine essence, and you to your feminine heart. Passion often suffers in second stage relationships. In a third stage relationship you nourish your feminine heart with love and daily pleasure in the body, you learn how to be an open channel of current emotion, and you show him your suffering when he collapses, and your pleasure and devotional love when he's his best self."

Denise: *"Yes, I like how this sounds, but I have no idea how."* "How do I learn how to do all this?"

Theo: "It's my job to help you."

Nancy is less explosive in her individual session than when she is in treatment with Don. One reason for this is that Theo is not jabbing her with challenging passive-aggressive shots like Don reflexively does, but instead is opening her with masculine presence. Another reason Nancy is more accessible is that her center of gravity, her most natural way of being when she's relaxed and open, is to be a charming, moderately self-reflective, egalitarian, pluralistic woman. Nancy doesn't see the irony of how offended and indignant she would be if she observed anyone treating herself, her children, or her friends in the ways she typically treats Don and the kids when she's in a defensive state. Additionally, Theo and Nancy are not intimate enough for Nancy's deepest defenses to be evoked. The more intimate we are with one another, the more deeply we can love, but also the more automatically we can enter primitive states when we feel threatened. A lover relationship or a family can thus be either heaven or hell on earth; depending on how true we are to our deepest sexual essences and how effectively we can love through our defensive states.

This exchange also reveals how Theo is beginning to help Nancy identify and be true to her feminine heart. When she let herself yearn for love instead of rage in frustration, Theo felt pleasurably drawn to her. Using his body as an instrument, Theo correctly identified her yearning as a feminine power that Nancy needs to cultivate to have a more fulfilling relationship with Don. Feminine yearning without attack is magnetic and is a central form of feminine erotic radiance. Nancy still has a masculine take-charge side that she needs to evoke to deal with responsibilities, especially in setting boundaries for the kids, but too much of that masculine energy to the exclusion of feminine warmth, love, yearning, and flow tends to make women sick in the same way a man feels sick if he betrays his principles or avoids finding and following a purpose that feels deeply meaningful.

Part of Theo's job is to help Don and Nancy discover and nourish these deep aspects of themselves to support erotic polarity, while at the same time discerning, taking responsibility for, and transforming their defensive patterns into states of healthy response. A central way he does this is monitoring the intrapersonal and interpersonal relationships of all the participants in the various systems and supporting healthy energetic polarities, which naturally harmonize. This can result in the secure, autonomous attachment styles that researchers such as John Gottman[36] and Susan Johnson[37] have observed in happy couples, with the added perspective of each individual cultivating harmony with all of his or her internal selves. Theo wants Nancy to soothe her rageful self, liberate her feminine heart, detach from Denise, and support erotic polarity with Don. To do this, Theo needs to activate feminine healing in caring for Nancy without agenda, and masculine healing in reaching for deeper understanding and supporting stronger resolve in all participants to create progressively better perspectives and actions.

Here are Don and Nancy the night after her individual session. She's been slightly withdrawn all day, thinking about what Theo said and about the last few years with Don, and is appalled by how rejecting and emotionally stingy she's been. At Theo's suggestion, they are taking a walk around the neighborhood and talking about their day. Don is somewhat amazed at Nancy's references to needing to cultivate her feminine side with him, but he enjoys it and is trying to be present in response:

Don: Uncharacteristically revealing. "I like how you are tonight, Nancy."

Nancy: Feeling a little flood of warmth. *"He looks good in that shirt."* She impulsively takes his arm and smiles at him. Don bends down and kisses her and both feel a surprising surge of eroticism. She says to Don, "You might get lucky tonight."

Don: He is inexplicably both turned on and put off by the remark, but remembering what Theo said about passive-aggressive remarks, bends down and kisses her again, and simply says, "That's nice."

This is a moment of erotic polarity between them. Nancy is leading with her warmth and femininity, and Don is responding with depth of consciousness by trying to feel into the moment and open Nancy instead of closing her. They both have been yearning for more moments like this for years, but have resisted them through ignorance, fear, and bad habits. When Don is unobstructed in his masculine, and clear in his current purpose (to open Nancy), and Nancy is relaxing into her body and feminine nature, a natural erotic polarity blossoms between them.

Endnotes

[1] Deida (2004)
[2] Assagioli (1965)
[3] Brizendine (2006)
[4] Ibid
[5] Gottman (1999)
[6] Johnson (2006)

CHAPTER FIVE

Development

Our birth is but a sleep and a forgetting
The soul that rises with us, our life's star
Hath elsewhere had its setting
And cometh from afar
Not in utter nakedness, and not in entire forgetfulness
But trailing clouds of glory do we come,
From God who is our home.

~from *Reflections of a Young Man* by William Wordsworth~

Don and Nancy were each conceived in a sexual act of erotic polarity, gestated for nine months in intense, physical relationship with their mothers, and were born into a universe that was complicated beyond belief. Each continued bonding with parents after birth, and grew to discover their physical body was different from other objects (around five to seven months), to understand that they were emotionally separate from their mothers (around fifteen to twenty months), to consider the world a magical place that they or their parents could control (two to six years old), to learn that there were rules and roles they needed to embrace to feel included as members of their respective families and other important groups (six to eleven), to discover they had their own paths that were sometimes separate from their families (eleven to sixteen), and to establish adult identities that involved a plethora of drives, dreams, fears, relationships, and responsibilities (from teen years onward).

Along the way, both developed cognitively from literally thinking with their bodily experience as infants (called cognitively sensorimotor), to thinking magically and nonrationally as toddlers (cognitively preoperational), to thinking in either/or, concrete linear fashion as elementary schoolers (concrete operational), to being able to hold opposing concepts simultaneously and have self-reflective capacities as teenagers and adults (formal operational).

Morally, both started out as egocentric toddlers and children, grew in elementary school to Nancy believing her friends and family deserved care and Don believing that his friends and family deserved rights, and then further developed through high school to Nancy believing that everyone deserved care and Don believing that everyone deserved rights.[1]

Psychosexually, both grew from simple awareness of bodily pleasure, to awareness of erotic feelings, to Nancy yearning for love and fullness, and Don yearning to penetrate and possess the feminine. This eventually led them to romantic infatuation with each other, and to bonding as a couple in the heart of a family.[2] Their next psychosexual step—consciously pursuing love by being true to and developing their deepest sexual essences in erotic polarity with each other—was never taken, and Don's affair and Nancy's bitterness are two consequences of that lack.

Now Don and Nancy are the heads of a family with eleven-year-old Michael beginning to leave his conformist childhood and explore adult authority and interpersonal sexuality, and with fifteen year old Julie rebelling against her perceptions of family and cultural hypocrisy while she bonds with other wounded teens hungering for meaning and joy in what seems to be a dark world.

All four family members have central worldviews that are unique to them but similar to other individuals with their life conditions. Don has men friends that are dedicated to their families but also cheat on their wives with prostitutes or secret affairs. Nancy has women friends that take great pride in their appearance, children, and lifestyles but who also habitually trash their husbands as a cultural norm. Julie's friends normalize keeping secrets of all sorts from parents and viewing the world as a negative corrupt place, and Michael assumes that the less he thinks about his feelings and talks about them to his family, the better.

If these four grow, all the different cultures they are embedded in (including family, school, work, and friend cultures) will react to them shifting their worldviews. Some reactions will be positive and supportive, and some will subtly coerce them to go back to old ways of perceiving and acting.[3] Theo knows this, feels the presence and influence of all these shifting relationships, and realizes that, as the family grows, part of his job is to help each member, and the family as a whole system, deal with the cultural consequences of developmental shifts.

Julie gets busted

It's Tuesday morning at 10:00, and Julie and her best friend Heather are alone in Julie's room, smoking a joint. They have skipped school, Don's at work and Nancy's at the tennis club for her weekly doubles match, so the girls are home alone feeling a delicious, transgressive sense of forbidden pleasures. Both are dressed in full-on black Goth with lots of chains. Heather has piercings in her lip, nose, navel, and eyebrow along with conventional earrings. Nancy has, so far, prevailed in preventing Julie from similar piercings:

> Heather: Feeling disinhibited from the pot and noticing a note Nancy has left reminding Julie to clean the bathroom. "What's with your mom? Is she some kind of neat freak?"

> Julie: Pleasantly spacing out staring at the rosebush outside her window, she finds it jarring to be reminded of the person she fights with the most. "Fuck her. She's such a hypocrite. She's a bitch to everybody and wants me to be all sweet and nice."

> Heather: Giggling a little at the obscene references, but— being a feminine person—she responds in a somewhat caring way. "Your mom should smoke weed. It would mellow her out."

> Julie: Laughing at the image of her perfect, controlled mother smoking pot. "Right, and then we'll all take mushrooms together and go to the beach." This sends the girls into hysterical laughter for the ninety seconds it takes Nancy, whose tennis match was cancelled, to pull into the driveway, come in the front door, hear the girls, and walk down the hall to Julie's room. Nancy

dramatically flings the door open to be met with billows of pot smoke and the girls laughing on the bed. She freaks out as they look up, appalled.

Nancy: Directing her rage first to Heather. "You go home and tell your mother what you've been doing. Don't lie, because I'm calling her right after I have a few words with Julie."

Julie: Protecting her friend. "Come on Mom! Leave Heather out of this. This is between us."

Nancy: Turning toward Julie as Heather makes a quick exit. "Leave her out of this? She's skipping school, using drugs with my daughter, and she's just a child. Are you crazy? This is it. You are so grounded. Haven't we taught you any values?"

Julie: Defiant, and too stoned to have any caution with her mother. "I know about Dad and Denise. Don't talk to me about values. He cheats on you and you treat him like shit. What kind of values are those?"

Nancy: Overwhelmed with this blast, bursts into tears. "I don't know what to do."

Julie: Feeling sympathy and a little guilt at the unexpected tears, and realizing that she has broken a family taboo by referring to the affair. "It's OK Mom."

One of the main purposes of healthy families is to support development in all members. From conception to death we are evolving on a variety of developmental lines including the physical, interpersonal, psychosexual (both masculine line and feminine line in all people because we have both aspects), moral, values, cognitive, and any number of other lines that can be specific skills or abilities such as sports, dance, music, math, or art. Interestingly, the higher—or deeper—we are on any developmental line, the more there is a felt sense of spirituality.[4]

Our self-line is a weaving together of our values, interpersonal, moral, cognitive, and psychosexual lines the way the strands of a rope are woven together. Combined with our subjectively timeless and unwavering sense of personal identity, these lines cumulatively determine our sense of self; the person we experience looking out through our eyes at any given time. This self, or observing ego, is both the unchanging "I" that we subjectively have always been, and the changing "I" that is always developing and adapting in response to ever shifting relationships within ourselves and with the world.

Since development is include and transcend, we never lose our capacity to be any self that we've been. The screaming infant, the egocentric toddler, the earnest conforming third grader, the rebellious teen, and the confident (or anxious and self-doubting) young man or woman are all in us, ready to be evoked by life circumstances.[5] Often, under stress, we regress defensively to more primitive levels on different developmental lines. Under the right circumstances we can also have peak experiences of enhanced functioning.[6]

In the above example, Heather and Julie both began their dialog on the selfish level of moral development, pre-conventional in that they were more interested in gratifying their impulses than in conforming to the rules or evaluating what's in the highest good. The danger of oppositional teen subcultures like the drug using/ Goth dressing group that Heather and Julie belong to is that they can form tribes that normalize self-destructive and other-destructive behaviors. Gangbangers are an extreme example of this. There is a moral code, but it is a primitive one in which destructive behavior like teen drug use is normalized, and members of "our" group have rights that outsiders don't. In hunter-gatherer tribes this is frequently reflected in their languages where the word for "human being" means a member of our tribe, and there are different words that signify other non-tribe members as being less than, or at least different from, human beings.

Nancy's natural moral level (when she's not in a defensive or regressed state) is somewhat post-conventional. When relaxed and open, she believes that there are relative moral standards where rules sometimes should be broken for the higher good in service of deeper principles. Similarly, when open and unstressed, she believes that people should always be treated with respect, no matter what they're doing.

Under the shock of walking in on her daughter skipping school and smoking pot, Nancy's moral level regresses to a pure conventional level. Julie and Heather are breaking rules, and not only do they need to be punished, but their rule breaking behavior warrants contempt, condemnation, and blame. The added stress of Julie flinging Don's affair and Nancy's emotional abuse of him in her face shuts down Nancy's systems completely and she regresses and bursts into tears; not a bad alternative under the circumstances, since it provides Nancy with some emotional release, evokes some empathy in Julie, and temporarily avoids Nancy seeking relief by hammering someone she loves (one of her most destructive defensive habits).

Cognitively, when relaxed and open, both Julie and Nancy are formal operational, which means that they have the capacity to hold opposing concepts simultaneously in their minds and look from different perspectives at different situations. When stressed they regress to concrete operational thinking, where there is absolute right and wrong according to their version of the rules, and where there is only one explanation—rather than multiple perspectives—for situations like the one they find themselves in now.

Here is Nancy on the phone to Theo about the incident. She has already described the sequence of events:

> Theo: *"It's a little early, but it's time to work with the family. At least this gets Julie into treatment."* "I think we should have a family session."
>
> Nancy: Unconsciously resisting. "This would never have happened if Don wasn't off fucking that bitch. I hate it that Julie knows about it."
>
> Theo: *"Delicately. How close is she to decompensating?"* He uses a soothing tone and offers masculine direction. He knows that she is dangerously close to a state of diffuse physiological arousal, where heart rate climbs over one hundred beats a minute, and people can't easily see, hear or think. "You need to get a hold of yourself for your

family right now. Breathe deeply and soothe yourself. Julie might be in trouble, and we need to mobilize the family to help her. That means you can't go off on people when you get so angry. Your family needs you to keep a hold on yourself and stay present through this."

Nancy: Calming down. *"He's right, the kids need me."* "I don't think Michael should be part of this. He's too young."

Theo: Feeling a warm sense of appreciation for Nancy getting hold of herself, and a sense of affection for Michael. Both Don and Nancy have described him as a stand-up guy, who probably sees and knows far more than they imagine. Also, developmentally, at eleven he probably has more capacity than they realize for insight and self-reflection. Eleven is often where the cognitive fulcrum begins to tip towards formal operational (being able to hold conflicting perspectives simultaneously, and have more consistent self-reflective insight), and the moral line begins to have glimmerings of post-conventional values of care and rights for everybody in a complex non-rigid moral framework. "I disagree. Both you and Don describe him as a smart guy, and say he's tight with Julie. If she knows, he probably knows. He probably also knows about her pot smoking and who knows what else. I think it's time for the family to deal with this stuff."

Nancy: Revealingly assuming that Don has no say in any of this. "OK, I'll schedule an appointment."

Family therapy.

A family presents unique challenges to a therapist. Each member has his or her own constellations of defensive states and states of healthy response. Everybody is in relationship to themselves and everybody else in more or less self-regulating ways. This self-regulation (homeostatic self organization) supports the healthy functions of the family to cherish and support all members in their development, and the unhealthy functions of protecting individuals and the system from positive change. The system thus simultaneously supports healthy states and behaviors between members, and normalizes unhealthy states and behaviors.

Family systems welcome truth and growth and resist change to varying degrees depending upon their defensive structures. The therapeutic task is to find the event horizon that maximizes healthy growth without being so threatening that it drives the family out of treatment or an individual member into deep enough decompensation to compromise the treatment.

Here are Don, Nancy, Julie, and Michael in their first family session with Theo. Notice how he is constantly monitoring what he hears, sees, and feels to understand the individuals and the various relational systems the family contains. As the following session illustrates, distressed families will often devolve into triangles where members unconsciously create temporary alliances with different members to resist perceived threat.[7] The episode with Julie has just been explained and the affair has been mentioned:

> Theo: "What do you think of all this, Michael. Julie getting busted by your Mom for ditching and smoking pot, and your Dad having an affair with his office manager?"
>
> Michael: *"Why is he asking me?"* "I think it's pretty messed up."
>
> Theo: *"Keep him talking, it will open up the rest of them."* "What do you mean, 'messed up'?"
>
> Michael: "Julie and Mom fight all the time, and it seems like Julie doesn't follow any rules. And Mom and Dad never seem happy." He unexpectedly begins to cry.
>
> Don: Overcome with love for his son. "It's OK son."
>
> Nancy: Angry that her perfect family is not so perfect, and hurting seeing Michael's pain. The story she and Don always tell themselves is that Michael is just fine. "If you hadn't cheated, this wouldn't be happening Don."
>
> Julie: Her feminine heart feels the falseness of Nancy's attack, and, emboldened by the openness of the session, allies with Don against Nancy. "You are always such a bitch to Dad."

Don: Appalled at the violation of the family taboo against calling Nancy on her sadistic attacks, Don comes to Nancy's rescue. "Don't talk to your mother that way." Julie, feeling betrayed by her father, shuts up.

Theo: Feeling a tingle of irritation at Nancy for interrupting Don comforting Michael, and frustration at Don's rescue. *"You're being recruited into the system. This is what pressures all of them when they're stressed."* Observing how the family is organized to protect Nancy from having to acknowledge her shadow side of out-of-control anger, and Don from having to acknowledge his collapses away from responsibility to lead appropriately, he intervenes to open up the system. *"Nancy and Don are stronger than any of them realize. They need to stop protecting each other and start telling the truth."* "It's pretty dangerous to tell the truth about how you feel in this family."

Nancy: Offended. "I always tell it like it is."

Theo: Modeling to Don how to address her distortions. "Lashing out impulsively when you're angry without thought of what serves the highest good is not telling it like it is, it's self indulgence." This is followed by a hushed silence as everyone waits for the consequence of Theo breaking the family taboo against confronting Nancy in a mature fashion (it's acceptable to blow up and engage in immature attacks like Julie does routinely and Don episodically). Michael has stopped crying and the rest of the family has apparently forgotten his distress. Finally Don again comes to the rescue. His intent is positive, to lead his family and support his wife, but he can't discern between codependently supporting her distortions and offering healthy input. "Nancy's been through a lot recently."

Theo: Notices how Julie rolls her eyes. "You look like you have something to say, Julie."

Julie: "Dad never stands up to Mom. She dumps all over him and he just makes excuses for her."

Theo: *"She's treating Don like he's too fragile to handle criticism."* "Tell your Dad."

Julie: "You never stand up to Mom. You let her walk all over you."

Don: "We're trying to learn how to talk things out."

Nancy: "As if you were ever really interested in talking things out."

Julie: "That's just what I mean. Mom, you are so nasty to him."

Theo: Wanting to mobilize their strengths. "Nancy, tell Julie what's valid about what she just said."

Nancy: Really wanting things to be better in her family, and knowing she can't retreat into confusion or outrage with Theo present. *"What is valid about that? I do criticize him a lot."* "You're right I attack him too much. I'm working on that in our counseling."

Julie: This blows her mind. "You never admit you're wrong. You always blame someone else."

Nancy: "I just want us all to do well and love each other."

Theo supports this healthy dialog for about fifteen minutes, encouraging them to embrace ground rules of respectful relating, with special emphasis on Don and Nancy being responsible to discern and advocate for respectful tones. He is making structural interventions with the family, encouraging a healthy hierarchy of Don and Nancy being advocates of everybody's health and development, and responsible for insisting on caring relationships and emotional non-violence.[8] He is also indirectly supporting Don and Nancy's job of teaching the children to move from egocentric first stage relationships to more fair and communicative 50/50 second stage relationships. Finally, he brings it back to Julie:

Theo: "Julie, what are your personal guidelines for smoking pot?"

Julie: Instantly suspicious. All any adult has ever done is forbid her to smoke pot. No one has ever considered that she might have personal moral standards in this area. "I don't know what you're talking about."

Theo: He wants to open a channel for direct talk about drugs. He knows Julie is unlikely to stop smoking pot, and there's a strong possibility that other drugs are involved or will be involved in her life. Julie has never had a candid conversation with an adult about her pot use. All she has heard is pronouncements, rules, and prohibitions. To receive help in this area, she needs to learn how to discuss it with adults who care about her. Asking her what she feels is right and wrong strengthens her connection to the "we" in the room. "When do you think it's right for you to smoke pot, and when do you think it's wrong? I assume you don't think it's right to be stoned all the time."

Julie: Reluctantly. "I don't think it's right to smoke at school. I don't think people should drive when they're stoned. I try to not smoke more than three times a week." The rest of the family look at her with increased respect. Her demeanor and tone are adult and impressive. Theo elicits other values that Julie has. As it turns out, she is often a caretaker of her more rebellious friends, and Theo offers her some information about the difference between caring and codependence, and cautions her about pot.

Theo: "The statistics are that if someone smokes pot they are sixty-five times more likely to use other drugs. All drugs have the capacity to elicit addiction, which means using them in progressive or out-of-control ways. If you decide to continue pot, you'll find out what your tendencies and capacities are." There is uncomfortable silence after this. Everyone is thinking about addiction in one way or another. Theo lets this sink in for a few seconds, and then concludes this piece of work with Julie by asking her if she's interested in some individual sessions with Mary West.

Julie: *"Right, I'm the sick one. Fix me up."* "I don't need my head shrunk."

Theo: Laughing. Feeling a solid attunement with her and the rest of the family. *"If she has a drug problem, Mary could be a secure base to deal with it.* ""Julie, you are becoming a young woman. You are facing lots of important decisions and some, like ones involving sex, drugs, rage at your family, and important life decisions, are currently hard to talk about productively with your parents, even though you guys obviously love each other a lot. Mary is a smart woman who can support you and help you discover and develop who you really are."

Julie: Feeling a surge of longing for just such an advocate, she responds cautiously. "I'll try seeing her once and then decide."

Theo: "Good decision. Chemistry's important in therapy. If you don't like her, or feel she's not helping you, we can find you someone else." He feels into the family. Don and Nancy are obviously relieved and touched by the positive atmosphere and good interactions with Julie. They were dreading lots of pointless negative drama and it didn't manifest. Julie is interiorly focused and self-reflective. She's heard some mind-blowing material in this session. Michael seems somewhat detached from the family. His laid back style lends itself to being invisible with these other powerful figures. Theo's impulse is to pull him in closer.

Theo: "How are you feeling now, Michael?"

Michael: "Better."

Theo: "Better how?"

Michael: "I don't know. We just seem more together."

Theo: Wanting his worldview to be honored, encourages him to elaborate. "How are you more together?"

Michael: Uncomfortable being the center of attention, but liking that his opinion is being solicited. "I don't know. We're like talking instead of arguing. And Julie and Mom aren't all intense at each other."

Theo: With a smile. "You mean, like getting in each other's faces?" Everyone laughs. *"This is a good time to connect Don and Michael."* "Don, tell Michael how you're feeling about him right now."

Don: "I'm proud of you son. You've really helped this session be a good one." Michael glows in response, and Julie and Nancy are visibly touched by the exchange.

Theo ends the session by scheduling another family meeting in three weeks. Julie has agreed to see Mary West, and Don and Nancy are already scheduled for weekly conjoint sessions.

Endnotes

1. Wilber (2000)
2. Witt (2007)
3. Wilber (2003)
4. Wilber (2000)
5. *Ibid*
6. Witt (2007)
7. Nichols (2007)
8. *Ibid*

CHAPTER SIX

Love Always Involves Suffering

Pink floating clouds were exploding
Why are we angry on such a sweet night?
You've got your version and I've mine
Hey look, I apologize

~from *Fallen*~

Love and intimacy always involve pleasure and suffering. The pleasure is usually pretty easy to accept. The suffering is more problematic. Intimacy evokes our deepest capacities for joyful communion, and our darkest defenses against change and threat. The more integrity and care we bring to our intimate relationships, the clearer our path when suffering shows up. The more egocentric and selfish we are in intimacy, the more confused and destructive we tend to be when suffering intrudes.

People tend to attract and be attracted to their reciprocals. We are drawn to each other's dreams and wounds. To the extent we are wounded, we will attract and be attracted to complementary wounds. Bullies are drawn to victims who are often drawn to bullies. Unresolved men tend to be attracted to women conflicted about fully opening their feminine hearts who, in turn, tend to be attracted to unresolved men. We consciously and unconsciously seem to go for people who complement our dreams of love, success, and family, while also complementing our wounds and shadow.

The following session is the first session involving Denise and Dr. Harvey McBride, the psychologist that Theo referred her to. It is four weeks since Don broke up with her, and in that time Denise has found another job at a law firm in town. At this point in the session Denise has already filled Dr. McBride in on the arc of her relationship with Don. Her current dilemmas are largely centered around self-care and love, two common organizing principles of psychotherapy, and especially with clients who have a more feminine essence. Harvey's office is on the bottom floor of a Santa Barbara office building. There are two leather couches, a few chairs (Harvey does groups as well as individual and conjoint sessions), a desk, and only one window that looks out on a walkway:

> Denise: "I can't eat. I have trouble sleeping. All I can think about is Don. If it wasn't for his kids, he'd be with me."
>
> Harvey: Admiring her yearning, and feeling the intensity of her loss. "You're grieving, Denise. Your body, mind, and spirit are slowly digesting and integrating a major loss. Elizabeth Kubler-Ross said that grief is, alternately, denial, bargaining, anger, depression, and acceptance. It sounds like you've been experiencing all of those."
>
> Denise: "I just don't see why he would choose her. He said he loved me."
>
> Harvey: Energetically holding her and focusing on staying attuned. Understanding the feminine worldview that love is the most important thing, and suspecting that choosing principle over love is what pulled Don away from this erotically radiant woman. To the masculine, integrity, deep purpose, and freedom are often more important than love. "Now you're bargaining, trying to change the past by debating it. I'm sure he did love you and is grieving for you now."
>
> Denise: Genuinely bewildered. "How could he not choose to be with me? He said we had the best sex of his life, and he and Nancy practically stopped doing it years ago. I know he loves me and wants me."
>
> Harvey: Gently. "This is denial. From what you've said, Don will not go back to you."
>
> Denise: Back to bargaining, beginning to cry. "It's not fair. We were so good together." It continues like this for ten or fifteen minutes until, finally, Denise provides an opening for deeper exploration. "I never expected this to happen."

Harvey: *"How much responsibility can she take?"* "That's surprising to me."

Denise: *"Surprising?"* "I don't know what you mean."

Harvey: "You got involved in a secret affair with your boss who's married, has two children, is devoted to his family and is almost twelve years older than you. I tell my clients that, when they're choosing a lover, they should ask themselves five questions:

- Is there erotic polarity? Yes, there was lots of it with you and Don.

- Is this person self-regulating around their physical and psychological health? Don apparently hasn't arranged to be psychologically healthy in his marriage or in his relationship with you.

- If there is conflict, are they able and willing to do what it takes to get back to love? Don didn't do this with his wife, and now is not doing it with you.

- Would this person be a superior parent? Don sounds dedicated to his kids. I guess he's a good father to the extent that any father who cheats on his children's mother can be a good father.

- If the person is more masculine, do they have deep soul's purpose in their life, and if the person is more feminine, to they admire and support your deep soul's purpose? Don sounds dedicated to his business."

Denise: Somewhat defensively. "The answer to some of those is 'yes' with Don."

Harvey: "Have you ever dated a man where the answer was 'yes' to all five questions?"

Denise: Beginning to get it. "No. Are you saying I somehow set this up?"

Harvey: "The odds for any relationship turning into a life partnership are slim at best. The odds for this relationship were much worse. It seems a part of you believes that love will prevail even when the signs are terrible. Long shots hardly ever come in."

Denise: "But I love him."

Harvey: "What was your longest relationship before Don, and how did it end?"

Denise: "I dated Jack for three years but he drank too much and couldn't commit. He finally cheated on me and I left him."

Harvey: "What was your next longest relationship and how did it end?"

Denise: "I dated an architect in San Francisco named Charles. It was a long distance relationship for two years, and then I fell in love with Don."

Harvey: Smiling. "Are you noticing a pattern here?"

Denise: Interested in her process at this moment, and seeing her relationship pattern in a slightly new way. "After two or three years somebody is unfaithful and the relationship ends. I don't feel like I make that happen, but it keeps happening."

Harvey: "Well, one way you contribute is by affiliating with guys who are a 'no' on one or more of those five characteristics. Do you believe you deserve love from a healthy man?"

Denise: Begins to cry again. "I thought Don was the best man I ever dated." Harvey relaxes and watches her compassionately until she looks up and smiles wanly. "I guess it wasn't a good sign that he was willing to cheat on his wife."

Harvey: Laughs. She is radiant and endearing, and Harvey feels a momentary surge of attraction and caution. He knows that such feelings mean he's probably projecting some idealized figure onto Denise, which is called positive countertransference in therapy (to distinguish it from positive transference, which is a client projecting an idealized figure onto a therapist). *"Watch out for countertransference, Harvey."* "Yes, I'd say that's a pretty bad sign. I think part of your work is to learn to better discern healthy guys, and to realize that certain kinds of unresolved men are attractive to you."

Denise: Suddenly curious, and, trusting Harvey at the moment, willing to ask for feedback about her self-destructive pattern. "Why is that?"

Harvey: *"Gently. There's something here."* "You said your parents divorced when you were young and your mother remarried. How trustable were the adults around you, especially the men?"

Denise: She looks away and her breathing rises up into her chest. "I didn't trust anybody really. I wouldn't live with my mother and stepfather. She's an alcoholic and he's a monster."

Harvey: He knows the probable significance of "monster," and a wave of sadness and compassion floods over him. *"It's so often the stepfather."* Was there physical, sexual, or emotional abuse?"

Denise: Finding it somewhat shocking to be asked outright about abuse. *"Just say it."* "My stepfather molested me."

Harvey: *"Help her tell the story."* "Tell me about it."

They continue for fifteen minutes as Harvey hears the outline of two years of terror and molestation until ten-year-old Denise finally creatively figured out a way to use her emotions to avoid going to her mother and stepfather's house.

Harvey: Warmly, admiring the courage of that fifth grade girl who somehow figured a way out of a nightmare. *"Help her create a new story where she sees how brave and beautiful she was."* "Good job stopping it when you were ten. Lots of ten-year-olds don't have the resources or courage to end abuse."

Denise: Feeling strangely better. It's soothing to be admired for something she did during the molestation that she's so ashamed of. "I should have told someone. I just couldn't. Becoming hysterical when they tried to get me to go to their house was the only thing I could do."

Harvey: "I have a therapy group that I think could help you, and that you could help. There are several molestation survivors in it. It's also less expensive than individual psychotherapy."

Denise: *"Scary, but he says it'll help."* "I'll try it."

Much of Denise's suffering has been inevitable because of her attraction to wounded men. Her relationships with her immature absent father, alcoholic mother, and abusive stepfather taught her to feel at home with wounded family members, and to not demand integrity or adult care in her relationships. She learned as a child to ignore the inner voices that cautioned her about egocentric or immature adults because her normal existence from birth onward always involved living with egocentric, wounded caregivers. Her work now includes learning to discern the differences between mature integrity and the immature willingness to surrender to egocentric collapse. Until the part of her than can discriminate health and set boundaries in service of her discernment is cultivated, developed, and trusted by her executive ego, she'll be doomed to feel "at home" with people (especially men) who initially admire and care for her, but who are likely to eventually desert or abuse her.

Michael has a crisis.

On the other side of town that night, Michael is at a sleepover at his best friend Alex's house. Since it's a school night, Alex's mother has insisted they go to bed at 9:00, but instead of sleeping, Alex crawls into bed with Michael and they start giggling and tickling each other. This progresses into genital caress and then into Alex enthusiastically going down on Michael. Alex is wired almost exclusively homosexual. He's always been attracted to boys, has never been attracted to girls, and has been sexually aware as long as he can remember. He has been the more active partner in structuring his and Michael's sexual relationship. Michael is wired mostly heterosexually, but he likes the closeness, eroticism, and pleasure of his and Alex's sexual play, while feeling vaguely guilty about it and trying to not think about it when they are not actively being sexual. Right now he's fantasizing about Julie's big-breasted friend Heather and surrendering to the pleasure of having his penis sucked by Alex. To his surprise, he has his first orgasm:

Michael: A little alarmed. *"What just happened?"* "Whoa! What's that?"

Alex: Laughing, excited. "You came man. It was cool."

Michael: "It's never happened before."

Alex: "No way. I've been coming for a long time. Now you suck me."

Michael: Repulsed. "I don't want to."

Alex: Frustrated and irritated, and so emboldened to be more sexually assertive than he's been previously. "Come on man, I sucked you off. It's my turn."

Michael: He doesn't want to be unfair. Fairness is very important to elementary and middle-schoolers. Developmentally, their either/or, black/white, mostly concrete operational worlds operate according to rules of fairness for members of important groups. On the other hand, he's still a little freaked out by his orgasm. New involuntary responses of any kind can be scary. Also, he's experiencing his first refractory period. After his orgasm, he doesn't feel that sexually charged, and going down on Alex wasn't particularly attractive to begin with. Suddenly, this is an important decision point for him. His moral standards say he should be fair, but he's also been taught to say "no" when he feels "no." He values his friendship, and is reluctant to risk it by frustrating Alex. He finally, accurately, concludes that a good friend would not want him to do something that feels wrong. "No."

Alex: *"It's not fair. Fuck him."* "Screw you then, I'll jerk off." And he proceeds to masturbate to orgasm, while Michael lies next to him feeling guilty and yet interested in Alex's technique. He's never been taught how to masturbate to orgasm, and, the more he thinks about it, the more he wants to experience orgasm again.

The next day Michael is somewhat uncomfortable around Alex, and Alex (who has been homosexually inclined in a homophobic culture for years) feels it and is irritable and distant as his mother drives them to school. Michael obsesses about the situation all day, but has nowhere to go with it. He is completely sure he doesn't want to talk to anyone in his family. Julie can be cruel, and his parents have made enough critical references to homosexuals throughout his life so that he doesn't feel safe talking to them. He finally has an idea and brings it up casually at the dinner table:

> Michael: "I think I'd like to go see Dr. Brown by myself." This pronouncement is followed by five seconds of silence.
>
> Nancy: Genuinely concerned. "What's wrong honey? You can talk to us."
>
> Don: "Yes, son. Are you having trouble at school."
>
> Michael: On the spot now and wishing he had just shut up. "Never mind."
>
> Julie: *"He really is a sweet kid."* "You can talk to me. I understand what's it's like to be a sixth grader."
>
> Michael: Beginning to get desperate. "I said, never mind!"
>
> Nancy: Irritated, and unconsciously ramping up her defensive, take charge masculine side. Right now, she wants more to solve the problem than to read into Michael's heart. "Come on Michael. You need to tell us."
>
> Don: *"Theo said I should say what I think is best for the family."* "No. Michael asked for a private session and I think he should have it. If he doesn't want to talk to us, that's fine. We're not going to force him. Alright son?" Julie is visibly impressed by her Dad's intervention.
>
> Michael: Looking gratefully at his Dad. Don has rarely noticed what he really needed and stood up to Nancy about it. "OK."
>
> Nancy: About to press, but noticing that Don sounded strong and mature making the assertion. *"Dr. Brown said that when he acted in integrity, I was supposed to feel pleasure and show it."* She surprises and pleases the rest of the family with devotional surrender to Don's integrity. "You're right Don. I'm sorry Michael, we'll schedule you an appointment this week." Don looks at her. *"She really is beautiful."*

There is a lot of pain in these intimate encounters, but also much beauty. Don and Nancy are in states of healthy response and improved polarity. Michael is showing exceptional depth for a child of any age as he asks for an individual session. Julie feels more affection for her brother and more respect for her parents. The structure of the family is becoming healthier.

Still, there is pain. This pain is necessary and inevitable. Struggling to do right means enduring the discomfort of frustrating the parts of us that have impulses to do wrong. Initially, it is the easy way out to indulge an inner voice that tells us to avoid important issues, but eventually it leads to increased suffering. Trying to do right also creates pain, but pain in the service of health and development. Having intimate friends, lovers, and family members means regularly encountering the pain of conflict, misunderstanding, and challenges to grow.

Three days later, Michael is sitting in Theo's waiting room looking at a surfing magazine as the door opens. He's masturbated to orgasm several times since his encounter with Alex, and, though embarrassed, enjoyed it. He's nervous, but resolved to talk about what happened:

> Theo: *"He looks nervous, I hope it isn't drug addiction or abuse. Don just doesn't feel like he'd harm a child."* Theo knows these are worst-case scenarios that he's generating in response to his concerns for Michael. He centers, breathes deeply, consciously soothes himself, and gets dialed into the right attitude to attune himself with Michael. *"Slow and relaxed, Theo."* Looking at the cover of the Surf magazine, which features Kelly Slater styling in a huge barreling wave in Indonesia. "I can't believe how big that tube is. Hey Michael, come on back. Can I get you some tea or water?" Michael gets settled into a chair with a cup of peppermint tea. Theo chats about surfing with him for a few minutes, and Michael begins to visibly relax.

Theo: *"Time to get to it."* "Michael, your Mom said you asked for this individual appointment. That sounds like you have something specific you'd like to talk about."

Michael: "Yeah, well, it's about my friend, Alex."

Theo: Feeling a sense of relief. *"Probably not abuse, thank God, unless Alex is being abused by someone. Well, you've filed Child Protective Service reports before."* "I remember you saying he's your best friend. What's up with that?"

Michael: "This thing happened." Michael, with Theo's encouragement, proceeds to tell the whole story.

Theo: Feeling intense admiration for Michael asking for help with these difficult issues. "Congratulations."

Michael: Confused. This is totally unexpected. "What do you mean?"

Theo: "You had your first orgasm. There will be thousands more in your life. And as an added bonus, you learned how to masturbate, an important skill. How did you like orgasm?"

Michael: Uncomfortably. "I liked it a lot. But it was weird with Alex."

Theo: "What was weird?"

Michael: "He was all mad that I wouldn't, you know..."

Theo: "Suck his penis?"

Michael: "Yeah. And I didn't want to. I don't want to. I don't want to be gay."

Theo: He knows that Michael wants to experience himself as normal good guy. Right now, he has a critical narrative about his sexuality, and he needs to deconstruct it and structure a new narrative that good and right to him. For an eleven-year-old boy, this reconstruction involves discovering that he can be the hero in his own myth. Theo takes a deep breath. *"Slowly, help him wake up."* "What makes you think you might be gay?"

Michael: Feeling somewhat desperate, so just spilling it out. "I liked it when he sucked me. I liked the orgasm. I like Alex, he's my best friend."

Theo: *"Might as well just tell him."* "Well, first of all, from what you've told me, you're almost certainly not gay. You like looking at naked women. You don't like looking at naked men. When Alex was going down on you, you were fantasizing about Heather's breasts, right?"

Michael: "Yeah."

Theo: "Gay men tend to be the opposite of what I said. They get off looking at naked men. They tend to sexually fantasize about men. There are some guys that can only be sexual with women and would never be interested in being sexual with another man under any circumstances, there are some guys that can only be sexual with other men and would never be sexual with a woman, and then there's everybody else in between. You sound like one of those heterosexual guys who are programmed to be sexual with women, but can have certain kinds of sex with another guy if you really like him a lot."

Michael: Totally relieved. He's some kind of normal. "What about Alex? He's never interested in pictures of naked women."

Theo: Cultivating Michael's depth of consciousness by encouraging empathy for gay men living in a society where many find them ugly and immoral. "I don't know. I'd have to talk to him. Maybe he's gay, or maybe something else. If he's gay he'll have to learn to hold onto himself as a good guy, even though he lives in a country that is somewhat homophobic. You seem to believe there's something scary, ugly, or immoral with being gay."

Michael: Uncomfortable being bigoted, but wanting to tell the truth. "Everybody seems down on gay people. My family makes fun of them. Kids at school tease each other saying, 'That's gay,' or, 'You're so gay.'"

Theo: *"Help him find his own moral compass, his own good."* "What do you think is right?"

Michael: Angrily. "I think people shouldn't be teased about who they are. If someone's gay, so what? Who does that hurt?"

Theo: *"Compassion for all beings. Let's not even be bigoted towards bigots."* I think the same as you. But that's hard when people around you, people you love, can be, how shall we say, a little bigoted?" He laughs and Michael briefly joins him. At this moment they both feel intensely morally correct. At eleven years old Michael is mostly conformist, where experiencing oneself as good is the same as feeling included in the group. This moment is a peak experience for him on the moral line and cognitive lines because he is deep enough to hold to a more widely caring moral standard than the cultures he's embedded in (school and his family). He is not only feeling accepting of gay people, he is feeling compassionate acceptance of (rather than contemptuous dismissal of) people he feels morally deeper than (homophobic children and adults). This is a mature, formal operational moment. He is holding two opposing concepts simultaneously and seeing the merits of both. "So, do you want to continue a sexual relationship with Alex?"

Michael: Shocked that Theo might consider this an option. "It's too weird for me. I think I don't want to."

Theo: *"Now, help him help his friend."* "Have you told Alex?"

Michael: "Do you think I should?"

Theo: *"I wish I knew if Alex's family was safe for him to come out if he's gay. One therapy session would give a good idea."* "Absolutely. He's your friend, and he deserves a clear message. When you tell him, it's important to not make him think that you don't like him anymore, or that you think he's messed up. If he's gay this will be scary for him."

Michael: "I don't care if he's gay, I just don't want to do it anymore. What do I say?"

Theo: "Tell him the truth. It was fun, but it was too weird for you so you don't want to play look, touch, and suck sexual games with him anymore. I also suggest you tell him about this session and encourage him to ask his parents if he could talk to a therapist. When you start being sexual with other people, there are some things you really should know."

Michael: "Like what?"

Theo: Relaxing. Sex education is pretty straightforward. Also, if he can give interesting enough information, maybe Michael will talk about the session with Alex and help him get into treatment to make sure he's OK. *"It's too bad there's no other ethical way to help Alex and his family more directly."* "You should really know how to choose good people to be sexual with, how to say yes and no, and also how to have safe sex."

Michael: "You mean, like condoms."

Theo: "You got it. Like condoms. I told my kids, choose nice people, have fun sex, and use condoms. Condoms aren't the only thing in safe sex, but they're important." *"How open is he to talking to Don and Nancy? They can handle this, they're in treatment."* "Michael, I think it would be good for you and your parents to talk about all this."

Michael: Alarmed. "You're not going to tell them?"

Theo: "No, but I think you should. They know more than you think about sex, relationships, and love, and I think it would be good for your family if you could discuss all this with them, even if it's just your Mom or your Dad alone. You could start in a session here if you wanted."

Michael: Feeling dread, but also liking the idea of not having to be so secret with sexual thoughts, feelings, and behaviors. "Maybe."

Theo: "I can't tell you how impressed I am that you asked for this session and had the courage to talk to me about all this stuff. Do you want to come back and talk with me some more?"

Michael: "Yes."

Theo is adapting techniques from narrative therapy as he works with Michael. He elicits Michael's story of his life to date, what story Michael—in his deepest heart—wants to be the hero in, and what's blocking Michael from living that new story. Then he guides, supports, and encourages Michael to live his new story. This involves helping him discern and own values that feel good, embrace the perspectives that feel beautiful, and consider information that seems true.

Doing this requires Michael learning how to better tolerate the pain that is inherent in all his intimate relationships, both intrapersonal and interpersonal. Michael's painful intrapersonal relationships involve the parts of him that are judgmental, immature, violent, unacceptable, or unattractive to his current worldview. The painful interpersonal relationships involve the difficulties he has with others. A central focus of therapy is to help clients tolerate these kinds of pain and reach for truth, love, health, and growth in all their relationships.

Endnotes

[1] Nichols (2007)

CHAPTER SEVEN

Defensive States

Sometimes you're all I think about,
Maybe I'm obsessed.
Pumping seratonin
To my hypothalamus,
O Yes.
It ebbs and flows.

Cause I was lying to myself,
How was I to know?
Yeah, lying to myself, baby
How was I to know?

~from Lying to myself~

It's a fine Sunday Morning at 8:00 A.M. Theo and Sandy are walking on Arroyo Burro Beach. The air is cool and clear and the ocean roars with a four-foot autumn swell. A pod of dolphins a hundred yards off shore paces them for a few minutes. Theo and Sandy have been entertaining themselves identifying the couples walking on the beach that probably woke up, made love, and then were drawn to nature. These couples seem more pleasurably connected and physically close than others:

Sandy: She notices Theo turn inward and smiles. "Thinking about clients?"

Theo: Laughs, looks around, breaths in the ocean air, relaxes into the morning, and feels part of the beauty all around him. "It's a good thing. I had this outstanding session with a boy last month, his parents are doing well, it's time for a big problem."

Sandy: "Why's that?"

Theo: Their family system is shifting, and the deeper relational defenses are bound to act up soon. Somebody will decompensate in response to the changing system, unconsciously resisting the symbolic death and rebirth of expanding worldviews. The guy might collapse and cheat, the woman might collapse into a rage that can't be soothed, the daughter may collapse into teen self-destruction, or the son might collapse into deserting his new principles. You never know with defensive states exactly how deeply embedded they are. Neurotic and characterological defenses can look very similar sometimes."

Sandy: Laughing. "Boy, ask a simple question around here and watch out. Lighten up. It sounds to me like the family's doing fine."

Theo: Smiling. "You're right. Almost certainly they'll get through it better on the other side. Like I said, it's a good thing. It just means there's a particularly intense session on the way soon."

People regularly shift from one state of consciousness to another. We wake each morning and enter the gross state of waking reality where we are likely to identify with our name, body, family, profession, gender, and any number of other markers that we associate with who we are in the waking world. At night we go to sleep and enter a subtle dreaming state, and then sink into a causal state of deep, dreamless sleep. In the subtle dreaming state we can have a shifting identity that doesn't necessarily identify with name, body, family, profession, or gender. We can be or do anything. When we transition into a causal state of deep dreamless sleep we are consciously aware of no objects, and some spiritual traditions maintain it is in deep dreamless sleep that we are most one with the ever present witness that observes all objects but is itself not an object. Waking (gross), dreaming (subtle), and deep dreamless sleep (causal) constitute just one major framework that organizes states of consciousness.[1]

Another, related, framework is the different kinds of spiritually charged, transcendent states that are available to most humans. We can have transcendent states of deep awareness of, and/or identification with, nature (nature mysticism, often associated with gross, waking reality), deep connection with transcendent gods, goddesses, or spiritual entities (deity mysticism, often associated with dream states), expansion into infinite emptiness (causal states, often associated with deep dreamless sleep), and oneness with all that is, has been, and will be (non-dual states).[2]

We can have regressed states of feeling, thinking, and acting much younger than our chronological age, both healthy regressions as when we happily play like a child, and unhealthy regressions when we think and act in egocentric and destructive ways.[3]

Each state of consciousness involves energies that permeate and characterize it, and each constellation of energies—called "energy bodies" by some[4]--has exterior, externally observable aspects (like brainwaves, temperature changes, or neurobiological shifts), and interior, subjectively observable aspects (like feelings of anger, fear, joy, love, repulsion, unity, or transcendence).[5]

Psychotherapists have observed for over a century that clients move back and forth on a continuum with defensive states on one end and states of healthy response to the present moment on the other. Defensive states are habitual reactions to perceived threat that involve amplified or numbed emotions, distorted thoughts and perceptions, destructive impulses, and diminished capacities for empathy and self-reflection. States of healthy response to the present moment involve an individual doing his best, given current worldview and capabilities, to think and do what he believes serves the highest good, usually while maintaining some empathetic, caring connection with self and others.[6]

Therapy works to maximize states of healthy response where a person is attempting to do right while maintaining caring connections with others. During states of healthy response we tend to naturally utilize the beautiful, good, and true validity standards. In defensive states we tend to avoid consciously bringing all three validity to bear. We all have defense structures involving habitual tendencies of protection against perceived threat that are hard wired into our nervous systems genetically, congenitally, relationally, and through epigenetic processes where our experience helps structure the genetically programmed development of our body.

Characterological, neurotic, and relational defenses.

There are three major kinds of defensive structures: characterological, neurotic, and relational. All three tend to manifest as defensive states where we have amplified or numbed emotions, distorted perspectives and beliefs, destructive impulses, and diminished capacities for empathy and self-reflection.

The most dangerous and deeply rooted defenses are the **characterological defenses** that are often a result of not making it out of toddlerhood with an ability to have a clear sense of self when we are distressed. The defensive states that arise out of characterological defensive structures are particularly nasty because, when we are in their grip, we have practically no empathy for others—which makes it much easier to surrender to impulses to hurt people to get relief—and practically no ability to effectively self-reflect or self-soothe—which makes it enormously difficult to self-regulate our amped emotion and distorted thought. When sufficiently negatively aroused, it can be impossible to receive confrontation and feedback from other people. Diffuse physiological arousal—pulse above 100, and diminished capacities to hear, see, and think—is particularly hazardous when accompanying a characterological defensive state, because it amplifies impulsivity, and renders empathy and self-reflection even more inaccessible. When Nancy got so angry she didn't care who she hurt and wouldn't listen to anyone, she was in the grip of a characterological defensive state that involved diffuse physiological arousal.

Neurotic defenses often blossom between two and six as we expand language and conceptual skills beyond the capacities for internalized images, symbols, and beginning concepts. A central aspect of language development is the capacity to internally manipulate concepts. Children unconsciously use this capacity to deal with threat by repressing, suppressing, dissociating, projecting, denying, somaticizing or scapegoating threatening material. In other words, their self-protective instincts take scary truth and turn it into slightly less scary lies or avoidance.[7]

Neurotic defenses involve states that—while still driven by amplified or numbed emotion, distorted perceptions and thoughts, and destructive impulses—have some capacity for empathy and insight, and some ability to self-soothe and self-regulate distressing emotion in healthy ways. An example could be noticing you want to say something mean while rationalizing how the other person deserves it, and instead telling yourself more compassionate truth, breathing deeply to calm down, or seeking and receiving appropriate support.

Theo knows that Don and Nancy mostly have neurotic defenses, which respond well to uncovering in the light mature discernment. On the other hand, under the right constellation of internal and external stressors, either Don or Nancy can decompensate and enter characterological defensive states where Theo's clinical agenda needs to shift to containing, holding, and protecting them and others from harm while helping them rediscover empathy and self-regulation.

Relational defenses are defensive patterns that two or more people reflexively constellate cooperatively under stress. People together naturally connect in complementary intersubjective energy fields, and these connections can be more healthy responses to the present moment, or more defensive patterns. We each develop the templates for our side of defensive patterns through a combination of our inherent nature and learning (mostly anchored in relationships we have with family members), and then reenact them with others—especially intimate others—in complementary fashion that can eerily resemble patterns from our past.

The more we indulge defensive patterns, the deeper the defensive grooves become until we often feel like we have no choice in defensive patterns with strangers, lovers, friends, or family members. Relational defensive patterns can be any combination of characterological and neurotic defensive states. For instance, a driver is cut off on the freeway and, in a fit of impulsive anger, honks and flips off the offending car. The other driver can respond in healthy fashion (wave and apologize), neurotic fashion (honk and scream), or in characterological fashion (pull out a gun and shoot our first driver).

It is 11:15 on the Tuesday after Theo and Sandy's Sunday beach walk, and Don and Nancy are having their weekly session in Theo's office. This is their eighth conjoint session, and things have been going well. They've made love twice in the last four weeks, and they are having intimate talks two or three times a week that involve real appreciation and respect for each other. The quality of their healthy intimacy is deepening and the grip of their destructive patterns is loosening. There is still contemptuous attack from Nancy and passive-aggressive withdrawal from Don, but less than before therapy. After two family sessions and several individual sessions with Mary West, Julie has been slightly less oppositional, and Michael seems to have had good experiences in his two individual sessions, though he still hasn't talked to his parents about the content. Today, Nancy seems agitated and easily irritated:

> Theo: *"Something's on her mind."* "Nancy, you seem on edge today."
>
> Nancy: *"This is such bullshit."* Bitingly. "I don't appreciate being lied to."
>
> Don: A sense of dread expands in his chest. "What do you mean?"
>
> Nancy: "What do you think I mean? I saw your phone log. You've been calling that whore."
>
> Don: Enters a passive-aggressive defensive state where he just doesn't perceive the real point. Gives a classic, second stage, 50/50 defensive offering, complete with self-righteous tone. "I don't check your phone messages."
>
> Nancy: Gathering momentum. "You called her four times."
>
> Don: "I don't see why you...
>
> Theo: *"Time to interrupt before this gets out of hand."* He decides to soothe Nancy, who at this point is shaking with rage, by confronting Don. In this fashion he

90

interrupts the relational defensive pattern by taking the job of dealing with Don's neurotic defensive state away from Nancy's characterological defensive state, and models dealing with distressing material in a compassionate fashion. "Don, you're avoiding the point. First of all, what's valid about you calling Denise? Second of all, what's going on?"

Don: Defensively. "She was my office manager for two years. I need to call her with questions about what she did."

Nancy: Scathingly. "Right."

Theo: *"Use it as an opportunity, if Nancy can tolerate it."* Staying connected to Nancy on a feeling level, literally feeling from his heart to her heart, and watching Don out of the corner of his eye, he speaks in a calm tone. "Nancy, I want you to relax, breathe, and stay connected from your heart to both me and Don while I talk to him about this. Okay?"

Nancy: *"Don lied to me again. I hate him."* She takes a deep breath, and considers what Theo just said. *"Theo's right. I should calm myself and deal with this."* She straightens up, looks at Theo, relaxes and breathes. "Okay."

Theo: Admiring her self-soothing. "Good job Nancy. Remember, feel what you're feeling, but stay connected. Now, Don, how did it feel talking to Denise?"

Don: Freezes. This is an impossible question for him. He is certain there is no honest answer that won't send Nancy into orbit. Don has increasingly organized his life over the last seventeen years to avoid, lie, or deflect away from material that might cue her rage. Now Theo is forcing him to either lie or risk evoking the part of her he has feared, adapted to, and accommodated throughout his marriage. His mind gets dense and confused. "What do you mean?"

Theo: "Did you enjoy talking to her? Did you have impulses to get personal? How did you feel after?"

Nancy: She hates this, and is cycling into a characterological defensive rage. She does not want to deal with the fact that her man claimed another woman, that another woman was able to give what she wouldn't give, and that she and Don created and maintained a family system where he could cheat and hide it for a year. She surrenders to the narcissistic impulse to demean and withdraw. "Fuck you Don. Take her then. You want her. Go ahead. Let's just get a divorce."

Theo: He recognizes her diffuse physiological arousal—pulse above 100, loss of abilities to hear, think, and see with her peripheral vision[8]--but also knows that a central aspect of her personal work is learning how to calm herself to a manageable level of emotional balance when she enters these states. In the absence of such self-soothing, she risks continuing to compulsively do violence to the people she loves the best when she's hurt past a certain point. *"What's her capacity to self-soothe and receive in this state?"* He focuses all his attention on Nancy, feeling into the hurt in her heart. He looks into her eyes to encourage her nervous system to harmonize with his caring state. He knows she has resonance circuits in her brain that will mirror his state of consciousness and register his intentionality if she feels safe enough.[9] He speaks as compassionately as he can. "Nancy, stop. Breathe deep into your abdomen. If you can't be in the room when Don discusses these things, then he and I can address them in an individual session. I still don't know what's going on, and, if we stay caught up in negative drama, we won't get to what's really happening." Theo notices Don breathing a little deeper as he hears this.

Nancy: Trying to get a hold of herself. She and Theo have talked a number of times about how her rage stops progress. She also is vaguely aware that she has previously agreed to not throw divorce into an argument and she just did. "OK, OK. I just want to get through this, and get that woman out of my life."

Theo: "Really good job, Nancy. I can see you breathing deeper, focusing, and trying to shift into a healthy state. Stay connected to my heart and Don's heart. So, Don, what was it like talking to Denise?"

Don: *"Fuck it. Tell the truth."* "I was really glad to talk to her at first, then afterwards I felt bad."

Nancy: Somewhat calmed down from her characterological defense of exploding and attacking, shifting into her neurotic defense of attack by analysis. "You knew it was wrong and you felt guilty, like a little boy."

Don: Feeling the sting and collapsing into his passive-aggressive fallback position of agreeing to everything. "Yes. You must be right."

Theo: *"Let's open it up."* "This is one of your classic relational patterns. Don, you're afraid of telling the truth so you lie by commission or omission. Nancy, like most feminine people you are energetically sensitive, so you feel something going on and check it out. You find the lie, and, rather than deal with the fact that you are cocreating a relationship where your husband doesn't trust you with the truth, you attack Don. You, Don, rather than ask yourself what you believe is in the highest good and will actually help you two get back to love, shut down and start organizing your behavior to placate Nancy. Nancy, since you never hear Don's opinion about what's in the highest good, you assume he has no depth and no opinions, and then you lecture him, or analyze him contemptuously. You, Don, know this doesn't help, but you're afraid of telling Nancy what you believe is best."

Nancy: Relaxing. "I'm not the only one who lectures."

Theo: Laughing. Feeling affection and appreciation for her. "Touché, but you have to admit I'm right about your relational pattern."

Nancy: "Yes. But does Don really have an opinion about what's in the highest good?"

Theo: "Ask him and find out."

Nancy: "Don?"

Don: He has been practicing asking himself what is best for everyone when he's stressed, and so he has more ability to do it now. He feels dense and speaks slowly and deliberately as people often do when they are struggling to shift from a defensive state to a state of healthy response. "I admit I still miss Denise. I try not to hurt you with that, Nancy, and I want our marriage to work. It was mostly business we talked about, but some of it was personal, and, frankly, I felt like a jerk. After all, I hired her, had the relationship, and then broke up and encouraged her to leave her job. I felt sad after talking to her, and more distant from you when I got home."

Nancy: She hates the references to Denise, but is drawn to Don when he shows this depth. She relaxes a little into her own vulnerability, and enters a state of healthy response. "I just want it to be over, and things to be better with us."

Don: Feeling more warmly towards her. Wanting to help. "Things are getting better. It just doesn't happen all at once."

Nancy: Liking his mature demeanor. "I know."

This ebb and flow of defensive states is typical in psychotherapy. The lightning fast shifts from states of healthy response to relational defensive patterns happen often in conjoint sessions. Theo has to stay connected to himself, to each partner's inner relationships between various aspects of themselves, and to the intersubjective energy fields that are constantly shifting between all participants.

There were only two times in the exchange that Theo was genuinely worried about characterological decompensation; when Don was tempted to lie about his phone calls, and when Nancy was tempted to surrender to her defensive rage. As each partner met the challenge of their defensive states, held onto their more mature self and tried to push through to love, Theo fell back into opening them up and encouraging them to have more healthy and mature relationships with themselves and each other.

Whether neurotic, characterological, or relational, this is everyone's work with defensive states. Discern, hold onto yourself, reach for compassionate perspectives and caring action, and do your best to do right.

Endnotes

[1] Wilber (2003)
2 Ibid
[3] Witt (2007)
[4] Wilber 2007)
[5] Wilber (2003)
[6] Witt (2007)
[7] Wilber (2000)
[8] Gottman (2005)
[9] Siegel (2007)

CHAPTER EIGHT

Shadow Work

I've never stuck around before.
Why? I do not know.
Maybe I'm not self aware,
or does she drive me through that door?
I don't know.
It comes and goes.

Cause I was lying to myself,
how was I to know?
Yeah, Lying to myself,
how was I to know?

~from *Lying to myself*~

Don is with Denise again and they are about to make love. He is already anticipating holding and caressing her as they walk through a crowded gallery to a hotel lobby like the one in Pittsburgh at the insurance conference where they had two hot days together. Don feels guilty that he's cheating on Nancy, but he's desperate to find a private spot and ravish Denise until she screams in pleasure. Denise gets ambivalent and turns away from him and, in a sudden rage, he grabs her arms and swings her around. He sees fear and hurt in her face, feels intense self-loathing, and suddenly suspects that Nancy is somewhere in the lobby. He wakes up sweating next to Nancy and looks at the bedside clock. It is 3:00 A.M.

"Not again. Night after night. I can't talk about this with Nancy. Hey, Michael made an individual appointment with Theo, so will I." He immediately feels better and goes back to sleep.

Two days later he's sitting in Theo's office, telling him about the dream:

Don: "I'm dreaming like this two or three times a week. I can't tell Nancy. I know she'd think it was like I was still cheating on her."

Theo: Sees the shadow material (parts of Don that are hard for him to perceive) finding expression through the dream. There is hunger for Denise in Don's masculine desire for feminine erotic radiance, combined with rage at her for not being available. His moral standards tell him he should care about what pleases and hurts Nancy, who is somewhere in the lobby. There is unconscious implication that erotic bliss can never be experienced at home, but only in alien places. Theo sees this as a great opportunity to help Don acknowledge, process, and integrate shadow—those aspects of himself (both positive and negative) that Don has trouble perceiving and accepting. *"What a good dream."* "What do you think the dream means, Don?"

Don: He has a sudden guilty vision of Denise on a hotel room bed on her hands and knees, moaning in pleasure. "That I'm an asshole. That I just want Denise for sex."

Theo: *"We'll start with the moral standard."* "What percentage of the time you spent with Denise were you two actually having sex? You know, foreplay, intercourse, orgasm, the works?"

Don: Feeling some kind of masculine challenge. He's a numbers man. He can give a good answer to this question. He's surprised at how low his estimate is." Ten percent."

Theo: Impressed. Ten percent is an incredibly active sexual relationship, but he sticks to his original point. "It sounds like sex was plentiful and beautiful for you two. What did you do the other ninety percent of the time?"

Don: Relaxing, smiling at pleasant memories. "We drove in cars, we talked, we laughed, we watched videos, we went out to eat, and we hung out. Just normal stuff."

Theo: "What was fun about a those things?"

Don: "She was just so warm and beautiful. I enjoyed being with her."

Theo: "So, I guess the dream doesn't mean you only wanted Denise for sex."

Don: Somewhat disoriented being brought back to the dream, which defines his current relationship with Denise, an introjected figure that keeps reappearing to attract and frustrate him at night. "What do you think it means?"

Theo: He knows that most dreams are multidimensional constructs in which every part reflects some aspect of the dreamer. He also knows dreams often function as practice opportunities to work on real life problems. There are lots of ways Theo could work with this dream. Examples are offering interpretations from any of a variety of perspectives, having Don associate on different figures and themes, or asking Don to do any of a number of writing exercises. He decides to begin by using the classic Gestalt technique of encouraging Don to inhabit and relate with different dream figures and interactions, with the ultimate purpose of Don viscerally experiencing aspects of himself he is unaware of (or marginally aware of), and taking responsibility for owning and integrating those shadow parts into his larger sense of self. The organizing principles of Gestalt, pointing out the obvious, making the implicit explicit, and cultivating awareness as a healing experience, lend themselves well to acknowledging and healing conflicted intrapersonal relationships. "Close your eyes and go back into the dream. Be yourself walking with Denise through the gallery, and tell her what you're feeling and thinking."

Don: Feeling awkward, but, trusting Theo, he gives it a try, and speaks to an imaginary Denise. "I'm so glad to be with you. I can't wait to get to our room so we can make love. I wish it wasn't so crowded."

Theo: "Now, be Denise and respond."

Don: As Denise. "I love being with you, Don, but didn't we break up? You said you're working on your marriage. Should we even be here?"

Theo: "Be Don and respond."

Don: "You're right, we shouldn't be here, but I want you so much."

Theo: "Be Denise as she turns away."

Don: As Denise. "I don't like this, I'm going to leave."

Theo: "Be Don as he grabs her and talks to her."

Don: "Wait! I can't stand you leaving. I need you right now."

Theo: "Be Denise."

Don: As Denise. "You're hurting me. Stop this. It's just not right anymore." Tears form in Don's eyes. Theo instructs him to change roles.

Don: "I'm so sorry, baby. I miss you so much. God, the last thing I want to do is hurt you." Theo tells him to change roles.

Don: As Denise. Tears now brimming from his eyes. "Goodbye Don. I'll always love you." Theo waits patiently while Don quietly cries, and then instructs him to change roles.

Don: Letting her go, internally watching her walk out of the hotel lobby. "Goodbye Denise."

Theo: "What do you make of this so far?"

Don: "It's so hard to accept it's over. But the last time I talked to Denise on the phone, she told me to let her go and work on healing my family."

Theo: Knowing that Denise is in therapy with Dr. McBride. *"Good work, Harvey."* "How does that feel?"

Don: "Well, it's the morally right thing to do. You told me that it's probably the best thing for the family if Nancy and I can love each other better. But Denise is so beautiful."

Theo: "In the dream, is it the most beautiful thing to continue to be Denise's lover?"

Don: Remembering the dream Denise's look of hurt and fear when he grabbed her. "I guess not."

Theo: *"Time to bring Nancy in."* "Be Nancy, observing all this, and tell Don what you think and feel."

Don: Feeling a flash of anxiety, he resists. "But she wasn't in the dream."

Theo: Confronting. "You said that you suspected she was in the lobby of the hotel."

Don: Uncomfortable, but game. As Nancy he immediately feels a surprising rush of anger. "I knew it! I'll never trust you."

Theo: "Nancy, tell Don what you really want."

Don: As Nancy. "I don't want you to ever talk to her again. I want you to want me. I want you to take me into a hotel room and make love to me." He stops, startled by what he just said. Even though Nancy has told him many times she wants him to choose her, he's never really felt empathetic connection with her yearning to be ravished open erotically. It's kind of a sexy thought. He suddenly is aware that, when she's not contemptuous, Nancy's attractive.

Theo: *"I thought so."* "Well?"

Don: "Nancy doesn't like sex."

Theo: "That's not what she said last session about the lovemaking you two had the previous Sunday morning." Theo is suddenly distracted by the memory of Sandy walking with him on the beach and speculating on the Sunday morning sex couples. *"Focus, Theo."*

Don: *"It was really nice, but not like me and Denise."* "We have to work so hard at it."

Theo: "If you two could just keep improving a little at a time, the sky's the limit. That's one reason why couples in their fifties and sixties often report having the best sex of their lives.[1] Their biochemistry is not as charged, but they've learned how to open each other to deeper bliss through love, trust, practice, compassion, and depth of consciousness."

Don: Feeling affection for Nancy, and a little hopeful. "I wish we could."

Theo: "Go back into the dream and tell this to Nancy. See her in front of you in the hotel lobby."

Don: "I want us to be closer and have good sex, Nancy. I like it when we love each other." Theo directs him to change roles.

Don: As Nancy, feeling a bloom of eroticism. "We are in a hotel, Don." Both laugh and Theo pumps his fist saying, "Go, Nancy."

Don: Returning to a disturbing dream image. "I don't like it that I grabbed Denise and scared her in the dream. In other dreams I've hit her and yelled at her."

Theo: "What bothers you about all that?"

Don: "Isn't it obvious. I'm being an abusive creep."

Theo: *"Is he ready to go deeper?"* He offers an interpretation. "Right now you are passive-aggressively avoiding taking responsibility for your shadow."

Don: Inexplicably feeling caught doing something wrong. "What do you mean?"

Theo: Teaching, reaching to inspire Don to deeper consciousness. "We all have shadow parts we can't see or don't want to see. James Masterson once said that health is taking responsibility for everything we experience and do.[2] Taking responsibility for shadow means working at perceiving, accepting, and caring for those aspects about ourselves we resist acknowledging. Taking responsibility for shadow means protecting ourselves and others from destructive impulses that can arise in us, and integrating all our interior aspects into our whole self."

Don: "So the angry part of me is a shadow part?"

Theo: "Exactly. You feel it, despise it, deny it, or call yourself a creep, and it comes out indirectly in dreams or in passive-aggressive impulses and behaviors that don't feel hostile, but are hostile and cause suffering."

Don: Unconsciously mimicking Nancy's contemptuous tone. "What, so I should be going off on people like Nancy goes off on me?"

Theo: Laughing with pleasure. It's a peak experience for a therapist to participate in a client's awakening. "Right here is your distorted perspective; your belief that you have to either you go off on people, or suppress anger until it leaks out passive-aggressively. There are other options. Treat anger like any other painful experience; feel it, acknowledge it, act on it, and let it go. That's the way to integrate your angry self as a resource to help you serve yourself and others better."

Don: This feels true, and, like most masculine people, he likes having specific directions about the right way to do things. "Feel it, acknowledge it, act on it, and let it go. FAALG." They both laugh briefly at the acronym.

Theo: *"Bring Nancy back."* "There's more shadow material in your dream than just the way you've pathologized your anger. Notice how you've resisted viewing Nancy as an erotically radiant woman who wants to be ravished open by you."

Don: "How is that shadow?"

Theo: "In these last years, you've focused on how much you've suffered losing an erotic relationship with Nancy, and passive-aggressively avoided noticing how she's been yearning for a trustable masculine partner to love her open romantically and erotically. Look at the books she reads, Nora Roberts and Georgette Heyer; they are all about secretly yearning women being claimed in every way by trustable men. Part of her anger at you is that you haven't noticed, acknowledged, or claimed the yearning that is such a central part of her. She is an erotically radiant, deeply feminine woman."

Don: "So shadow isn't only angry stuff?"

Theo: "Shadow is anything about you that you resist perceiving, acknowledging, loving, protecting, and integrating into your deeper self. It's your angry side, your wimpy side, your sexually aggressive side, the strengths you won't acknowledge, the memories thoughts, and impulses you are ashamed of, and the side of you that gets clueless and dense when you're threatened instead of stepping up and dealing with the situation." Don suddenly remembers the episode at dinner where he stood up for Michael's right to have a private session. At this moment, he gets it. Theo sees his look of knowing and presses on, wanting to anchor this progress in the family system. "I suggest you tell Nancy all about this."

Don: Totally alarmed. "She'll freak out."

Theo: "Anchor yourself in your resolve to have progressively better love with her. Treat her like the partner you want her to be, and then stand unrecoiling in the face of whatever happens. Just love her and remember that it's in everyone's best interest for your love affair with each other to blossom. If she goes into rage and can't get out of it with your loving attention, take a walk and then try again."

Don: "What about these dreams I keep having."

Theo: Confidently. He's been over this ground many times in the last thirty-five years. "When you wake up, stay in bed for a few minutes, go back into the dream, and be the different parts talking to each other like we did today. It will change everything."

There are as many ways of dealing with shadow as there are healing systems. Dreams are particularly useful because they automatically present us with what we deny and resist in symbolic form. Any activity that supports discerning, accepting, and being responsible for aspects of ourselves we resist perceiving is shadow work. Defensive states are wonderful windows to shadow. If we soothe amplified emotion (or let ourselves feel numbed emotion), challenge distorted beliefs, resist destructive impulses, and reach for caring perspectives and actions, we are using defensive states to grow instead of to resist change. This is lifelong practice, and is especially necessary for therapists since it's hard to trust a teacher who doesn't live the principles he or she teaches.

People are so complex and multidimensional that all of us have the capacity for almost any aspect of human functioning from the most selfish and self-destructive to the most transcendent. People tend to deny, be ashamed of, or be guilty about their less attractive beliefs and impulses (or occasionally their most attractive beliefs and impulses as when someone refuses to acknowledge strengths, success, or beauty). Problems arise when we neglect our work of being responsible for everything we experience and do. The way to be responsible for our shadow side is to discern shadow when it manifests, acknowledge shadow material, protect ourselves and others from potentially damaging perspectives and impulses, and then integrate shadow sides into wider, deeper, more compassionate understandings of ourselves and others. This helps us deepen as individuals and love better.

That afternoon, Don comes home early from work to find Nancy in the garden planting flowers. Both kids are off with friends, and, to Nancy's surprise, Don puts on comfortable clothes and joins her digging and planting. He tells her about his session and, as he predicted, she gets hurt and angry about his dreams:

Nancy: "If you want her so much, go to her."

Don: He reflexively recoils, but remembers that his mission when he is around her is to open her with his integrity and love. *"Acknowledge her yearning."* "Nancy, I'm truly sorry I hurt you, and I'd change it if I could. But it's in the past, and now all I can say is that I want you. Theo said you've suffered because I haven't believed that you want me as a lover."

Nancy: Deeply touched, but frightened of showing her vulnerability. She clings to her anger to avoid the danger of trusting him. "Theo just told you to say that."

Don: "I wouldn't say it if I didn't mean it. I know I need to grow, and it will take time. I think we would do best if we grew together."

105

Nancy: Drawn to him as he speaks from his heart. He puts his arms around her and kisses her. She smiles. "Keep that up and you might get lucky."

Don: In a transcendent moment, he smiles and says confidently. "Keep this up and you might get lucky." He takes her hand and leads her to the bedroom. She finds it erotic to be led, and, as she stands nuzzling him while he takes off her clothes, she gets progressively more turned on. They become passionate quickly, and Nancy finds herself hungry to be penetrated and filled up. As he enters her she becomes more abandoned, moaning and moving, and finally shocks both of them by saying, "Please, Don. I want you inside me now." Don is excited by her passion, stays connected to her heart and rides her energy, hungry for her pleasure. Nancy, for the first time in two years, comes during intercourse, pushing Don over the edge into his own orgasm.

This episode illustrates how integrating shadow material is often necessary for deep eroticism and love. To the feminine, presence, integrity, humor, and shadow tend to make masculine figures trustable and erotically attractive. To the masculine, a woman that can open herself up to express love through her body in response to his best self is erotically and emotionally desirable. To improve his marriage, Don needs to perceive, accept, and care for the shadow part of himself that runs from Nancy and resists taking on the responsibility of opening her to pleasure and love in their sexual relationship. Nancy needs to perceive, accept, and care for the shadow part of herself that automatically chooses anger over vulnerability, and embrace her responsibility as a feminine partner to notice when her man is acting from his heart, and show him her pleasure. As they both do this, love and eroticism blooms.

Shadow is present in all of us, young and old. The following exchange between Michael and Nancy happens later that evening as she kisses him goodnight. In many families, goodnight rituals are a time when children relax, are in intimate contact with parents, an—in the safety of embrace—allow shadow material to percolate up from their unconscious. Nancy is kissing Michael goodnight and telling him she loves him. As a result of the emotional and erotic intimacy of the afternoon she, unknown to herself, has opened somewhat and is projecting more warmth and femininity that she customarily does. Michael feels this and instinctively responds by feeling closer and more vulnerable than usual. He looks away and seems sad. Nancy catches this signal:

Nancy: "What is it sweetheart? You look worried."

Michael: Gathering his courage. "Are you and Dad going to get a divorce?"

Nancy: *"Where did he get that idea?"* "No." She smiles, thinking of the afternoon. "We're doing fine right now. What makes you ask?"

Michael: "Alex told me his parents are getting a divorce. And you and Dad fight all the time. I heard you talking about divorce last June. I don't know what to think."

Nancy: "Your father and I have not been doing well for awhile, but we're working on it and making progress. You don't have to worry about us divorcing."

Michael: Feels a tremendous sense of relief. It's so intoxicating that he goes further. "There's something I've been meaning to tell you."

Nancy: Feeling very intimate and loving. "What is it honey?" Michael proceeds to tell her the entire Alex saga, including what he discussed in his sessions with Theo. It blows her mind, but she has the presence to listen quietly until he is done. "What did Theo say again?"

Michael: "He said I should talk to you and Dad about it. He says I should give you a chance to help me with stuff like this. Would you tell Dad?"

Nancy: *"What next?"* "Sure, sweetheart. He won't be mad or anything, but he'll want to talk to you about it himself."

Michael: Drifting to sleep. It has been soothing to talk to Nancy and have her listen compassionately. "OK."

Nancy: Looking with love and concern at her son. *"I should call Jenny and talk to her. Theo suggested Alex see someone. If Alex thinks his parents are divorcing, he probably should talk to a therapist about it anyway."*

The more relaxed, accepting, and non-alarmed we are, the easier it is for shadow material to surface and be dealt with. Nancy's loving, maternal side was often blocked by her masculine sense of responsibility to get things done, and lack of trust in Don. Part of her shadow was resisting knowing what a powerful resource her feminine warmth is to everyone she loves. Her lack of awareness of, and honoring of, the power of this feminine warmth was a loss to her family. Don's lack of awareness of and respect for his power and responsibility to evoke her warmth with presence, humor, integrity, and shadow was another loss that contributed to this deficit, not just to Don's detriment, but to everybody's. Nancy opening from a loving side she typically resisted helped Michael open from a frightened side he typically avoided, and gave both an opportunity to access shadow material in service of love and growth.

Endnotes

---

[1] Schnarch (1997)
[2] Masterson (1981)

CHAPTER NINE

The Goddess

I'm a bitch, I'm a lover,
I'm a child, I'm a mother,
I'm a sinner, I'm a saint.
I do not feel ashamed.

~from *Bitch* by Meredith Brooks~

Nancy is having an individual session with Theo. She discovered that she has difficulty discussing some of the things her family has been going through with her best friends. It's beginning to distress her that they seem generally down on their husbands. She is now occasionally as wide open with Don as she has been with her good friends, and it is somewhat disorienting to discover that she is uncomfortable commiserating with friends on how dense, insensitive, and contemptible men are:

Nancy: "Usually we kind of put guys down when we talk, but it's beginning to seem wrong. It's weird, I don't feel like I've changed; I feel I'm more myself"

Theo: "I often tell people that therapy is less about changing than about being more purely yourself. David Deida says that a full spectrum woman can be wide open from all her aspects, and that growth is often less about developing new aspects of self, and more about opening up to who you truly are.[1] It reminds me of a song by Meredith Brooks where she says she's a "bitch, lover, child, mother, sinner, saint."

Nancy: "I don't want to be a bitch."

Theo: "So, how can you be wide open, angry, and not a bitch?"

Nancy: "I don't know. Either I express my anger and look like a bitch, or I pretend I'm not mad."

Theo: "How was anger expressed in your family when you were growing up?"

Nancy: "We were always supposed to be the perfect family. My sister and I were not allowed to be angry."

Theo: "How did your parents communicate anger to you?"

Nancy: "My mother would get cold and send us to our rooms. My dad would get nasty, or explode once in awhile."

Theo: "What did you feel, think, and do when your mom got cold or your dad got nasty?"

Nancy: "I thought it was unfair. I guess I felt angry too. I would go to my room as a little girl." She smiles. "When I was a teenager I got right in their faces."

Theo: "You smile when you talk about getting in their faces."

Nancy: "It felt good to not take it."

Theo: "And to dish it out?"

Nancy: Uncomfortable now that her pleasure at exploding is being examined. "They had some old fashioned ideas, and didn't understand what it was like to be a teenager. I hated it when they would be smug or self-righteous, and, yes, it was liberating to not be intimidated anymore."

Theo: Smiling. "Sounds like you shifted from being the *intimidatee* to being the *intimidator*. How does it work with them now?"

Nancy: "They only come over on holidays, and we all kind of stay polite and on the surface. I wanted my family to communicate better when I had kids."

Theo: *"How do you want love to work, Nancy?"* "How do you wish your parents would have dealt with anger when you were a child?"

Nancy: "Express it, but not be nasty. Work it out so everyone feels better." She sighs.

Theo: *"This is what she yearns for."* "You sigh."

Nancy: "When Don or Julie and I get mad it deteriorates so fast. Don takes off, Julie gets nasty, and I'm a bitch."

Theo: "When a wide open woman is angry in service of love, it can be a beautiful thing."

Nancy: "But how do you do that?"

Theo: Relaxing as he leans into this part of the session. The most difficult therapeutic task, stimulating Nancy's genuine yearning to serve love even when she is angry, has been accomplished. Now his job is to teach, interpret, and direct her into opening as a full spectrum woman who can serve love from all her emotional states. "If you stay connected to another's heart when you're angry, and focus on loving through your anger, good things can happen. The problem with anger is that it is difficult to stay connected empathetically to someone we're mad at. Like almost everybody, your parents blocked empathy when they were angry, and, to this day, it looks like they consider being emotionally expressive inappropriate."

Nancy: Getting it first with someone other than herself. "That's why Julie can be so sweet sometimes, and so cruel when she's mad. She loses her empathy."

Theo: "Yes."

Nancy: "I certainly have problems with empathy when I'm mad."

Theo: "When you're angry, stay connected to your heart, feel into the other's heart, and give love through your anger. A full spectrum woman can give love through any experience."

Nancy: Feeling into her heart, and extending out to Theo, and then to her family. "I need to remember this when I'm upset."

Theo: "I suggest you read Regina Thomashauer's books, *Mama Gena's School of the Womanly Arts*[2], and, *Mama Gena's Owner's and Operator's Guide to Men*[3]. You also might enjoy Denise Linn's book, *Secrets and Mysteries*[4]. I'll write them down for you."

Nancy: Remembering being bullied by her parents. "I still have to be able to stand up for myself."

Theo: *"The feminine grows best in the presence of loving praise."* "You've learned how to stand up for yourself. You became your own woman, not a construct of your parents' expectations and dreams. You have been doing a magnificent job of loving your family better while standing up for yourself more effectively when you're hurt and angry. These days you tend to more compassionately whack Don when he's not being his best self and, if he shifts towards being his best self, you sometimes have the capacity to notice and offer him devotional love. This is being the embodiment of the Goddess; channeling love through your body/mind/spirit into the world, no matter what you experience."

If we are wide open in first stage, egocentric fashion, we can become an archetype of selfishness, like many of the Greek Gods and heroes. If we are wide open in second stage egalitarianism, we seek independence and try to communicate our way through difficulties. In the second stage we often deny the special qualities of complete openness, and limit ourselves with iron adherence to rules of fairness we have unconsciously accepted as universal standards. When we are in a third stage moment, we open up fully to the love that we are, and let that love flow through us in whatever ways best open the moment.

In third stage service, we all exist in our own myths of transcendence that we can direct, interrupt, change or surrender to depending on what opens the moment. When we are completely open, we become archetypal figures for better or worse—gods and goddesses in our own epics. These epics can be selfish dramas if we live just for ourselves, self-limiting melodramas if we deny the special qualities of different personal paths, or transcendent myths if we live for the highest good.

A full spectrum woman can open from every point on the masculine/feminine continuum as the moment demands. In a third stage moment, she opens in the way that best serves love.

Most women, in their hearts, exist as Goddesses that yearn overwhelmingly to open as love without restraint, and offer that gift of love to the world.[5]

Julie is in her ninth session with Mary West. Therapy has been going well. They are in Mary's elegant office down a corridor in a two story Santa Barbara office building. As you turn right from the hallway into Mary's room, you immediately see a walled in Zen garden behind sliding glass doors. The sliders are open and the sprinklers are spraying water over the ferns, baby's tears, and sandstone rocks exquisitely displayed in traditional Japanese style. Sunlight on the rocks evokes peaceful feelings. Mary and Julie are seated on a comfortable couch, beneath an alcove where an alabaster statue of Kwan Win, a Chinese goddess of divine feminine compassion, looks across the Persian rug towards a portrait of the Dalai Lama on the opposite wall:

Julie: "I had this weird dream."

Mary: "Yes?"

Julie: "I put the cat in the microwave and turned it on. I didn't feel anything. What do you think it means?"

Mary: "Cat in microwave is angry. Not feeling anything means not knowing what you're feeling. Who would be most distressed by a cat in a microwave? Friend? Lover? Mother? Father? Brother?"

Julie: "My Mom totally lost it when my Dad found the neighbor's cat dead in the street. He had blood on his hands and she didn't know it wasn't our cat and she freaked."

Mary: "Angry at Mother. Not being consciously aware you are angry. Attacking her by hurting something innocent."

Julie: "I'm not hurting anything innocent!"

Mary: "Have you ever seen pictures of yourself when you were three?"

Julie: Begins to cry, at first not knowing why, and then slowly letting it all set in. "My Mom's gone through hell with me. I love her so much."

Mary: "It'd be good to tell her this."

Julie: "She'd just say 'I told you so' and lecture me."

Mary: "Perhaps, or maybe it would validate her in one of her most important feminine areas, being a mother."

Julie: "What do you mean, feminine areas?"

Mary: *"How cool she asks this question."* "What does it mean to you to be a woman?"

Julie: "I don't know."

Mary: "Who are the women you think are beautiful and cool."

Julie: She hesitates. "You mean, movie stars or people I know or..."

Mary: "All of them. Every one. Who would you most like to be?"

Julie: Struggling, searching out with her heart, until she gets a glimmer. "I'd like to be like you."

Mary: Temporarily distracted by how touched and honored she is by this statement. *"Don't get distracted. You know how tricky transference can be. Expand the projections."* "What about me would you like to emulate?

Julie: "I like your clothes. You seem happy with your family. I don't know, I like how you talk about things."

Mary: "This talking about deeper meanings is very important to you, isn't it?"

Julie: *"Feels so good."* "Yes. We can't talk about anything in my family without upsetting my mother."

Mary: "You know, two thirds of all human conversation is about other people. I think that's because we love each other so much. There are special qualities to all love. The way you love a lover, wanting him, wanting him to want you is a big one. Loving your parents and your relatives, and loving your friends are also intense. Perhaps the most global and responsible love is what a mother feels for her baby. A mother's love for her child is one of the most feminine loves there is. Your mother's love of you and your brother is a central organizing principle of her life."

Julie: Temporarily inspired by the vision of a full spectrum woman who could open as love to being a lover, mother, daughter, relative, friend, and person. "I wish my mom and I could share this."

Mary: "Talk to her. You might be surprised."

Julie: "You don't understand. She'd just start yelling or lecturing."

Mary: "Would you like to have a session here with her? Maybe I could help with that deeper level of connection that you yearn for." She notices Julie contract, and her breathing rise in her chest. "How are you feeling right now?"

Julie: "I'm scared."

Mary: *"Help her open. Theo said Nancy would rise to the occasion."* "Feel it in your body. Let it flow through you like water. Open to being scared of risking deeper sharing with your mother."

Julie: As she relaxes and lets the fear flow she feels glimmerings of her hunger to be more open with her Mom. "OK, I'll ask her if she'll come in next session."

David Deida maintains that women grow best in the presence of loving praise (while men grow best in the presence of loving challenge). He also maintains that women thrive in the community of other women.[6] Mary and Julie are a community of two women focused on the initiation and development of Julie. As they relax into Julie's life, it becomes obvious that it would serve the highest good for Julie and Nancy to join together more fully in community with each other. Mary has met Nancy at the beginning and end of sessions, and has talked with Theo about her, so she's reasonably certain that a conjoint session would be good for everybody.

Julie, Nancy, and Mary.

The following exchange is twenty minutes into the next session with Mary, Nancy, and Julie. Julie has just told Nancy that she doesn't trust her to share intimate secrets:

Nancy: *"I'm her mother. She should tell me everything."* "Haven't I always listened to you?"

Julie: Looking at Mary. She's learned to be wary of confronting her mother. Mary nods encouragingly. "You get mad and yell, or you ground me, or you lecture me. Why should I ask for that?"

Nancy: Deeply offended. "Well, what do you expect? You skip school, wear black, get stoned, and talk back all the time. You..."

Mary: *"She doesn't see the irony."* "Excuse me, but, Nancy, look at what you're doing right now."

Nancy: Confused, as people often are when directed into facing their defenses. "What? I'm just talking to my daughter."

Julie: In familiar territory, Her standard is, if Mom's being a bitch, she feels free to lash out. "Sure Mom, you know everything. You're never wrong about anything."

Nancy: Unconsciously relaxing into the swing of the relational defensive pattern. "Don't take that tone with me."

Mary: *"Get them talking about talking."* "If you two were at home, how would this conversation end up?"

Julie: Laughs ruefully. "I'd be punished." Nancy squirms a little at the truth of this.

Mary: "What do you think, Nancy?"

Nancy: On the defensive, she avoids the question. "What am I supposed to do? Let her talk to me in that snotty tone? Say, 'Sure, go ahead and get stoned and skip school, it's fine with me?"

Mary: "Ask Julie. She's almost sixteen. I'll bet she has some good ideas."

Nancy: This sounds so reasonable. *"Why don't I ever ask her?"* "OK. How should I be, Julie?"

Julie: Several sarcastic comments come immediately to mind, but she doesn't want to look mean to Mary, so she struggles to answer well. Though not conscious of it, she's reaching for an answer that feels moral and beautiful. "Well, you should use nicer tones with all of us. You get mad at me for my tone, but yours is just as bad." Julie is trying to establish second stage safety with her mother by negotiating predictable fair rules.

Nancy: *"That makes sense."* "OK, fair enough. What else?"

Julie: Digging into what really bugs her. "And you never admit you're wrong or apologize. It's always somebody else's fault or mistake."

Nancy: Struck by the truth of this. She falls back on the distorted perspective people often embrace in this situation. "I'm sorry, but that's just the way I am."

Mary: Using a loving tone. "Excuse me, but that's just the way your defenses are. It's a defense, a habit of closure, to avoid acknowledging a mistake and refusing to help repair it with an apology."

Nancy: Laughing in spite of herself. "That's what Theo says." All three laugh.

Mary: "Either we're both wrong, or you have some work to do. Maybe you could tell Julie how she could help?"

Nancy: Slowly, feeling her way through this unfamiliar territory. "If you would use a nicer tone when you tell me you think I'm wrong, maybe I could take a deep breath and, if you're right, admit it and apologize."

Julie: Doubtfully: "I'll try it. But you don't listen very well when you're mad."

Nancy: At this moment getting it. "I know I don't and I'm sorry. I'm working on it." All three pause as they realize that Nancy just apologized.

Julie: Relaxes and leans towards her mother as she hears this. "I'll try to not be nasty. I know I do it when I'm mad."

Mary: *"Time to support feminine pleasure. They both need it."* "Julie, what would be the most fun thing you could think of doing with your Mom right now?"

Julie: "For all three of us to go shopping and then go out to lunch." Nancy likes the sound of this, and smiles and nods.

Mary: *"Work a little on the transference."* "I'm sure we'd have fun, but therapists can't be social with clients. Why don't you two go out for shopping and lunch? The feminine is nourished by community with other women, and all sorts of pleasures like shopping, food, rest, massage, sex, play, color, texture, and laughter."

Nancy: "Why do you have to include sex? She's too young." Mary and Julie both start laughing. Julie says, "O, Mom!" Nancy continues "It seems like sex is all over the place these days."

Mary: "How is sex all over the place?"

Nancy: "Well, Julie wants to wear sexy clothes, and Michael had this sexual thing with his friend, and Don had his affair, and Don and I are, you know, getting it on more."

Julie: In real distress. "Whoa, too much knowledge, Mom." Now Mary and Nancy laugh.

Mary: "It's hard to realize that we're all sexual beings with our own sexual yearnings and relationships. Your Mom could help you a lot with yours, Julie. She's had more sex, in more different ways, than you and all your friends combined." Julie puts her hands up in mock protest. "Too much knowledge, way too much knowledge."

Nancy: "I would like to go shopping and go to lunch."

Julie: "That sounds nice, Mom."

There is a full range of feminine aspects reflected in this session. Growing with loving praise in community with other women, sexuality as a liberator and healer, pleasurable tones, non-violence and care in communication, compassionate embrace of children, embracing shadow, anger in service of love, and cultivating softness when it serves love in intimacy all are present. The feminine shadow aspects of immediate anger (not toxic residue, but appropriate current emotion), deep ravishment, overwhelming sensuality and sexual passion are especially important, but, although this session was a step in the right direction, Nancy and Julie need to be a lot safer with each other to be able to talk productively about such potentially explosive material.

The intuitive attraction of inhabiting the Goddess archetype is revealed in the shared understanding of Mary, Julie, and Nancy that opening on all channels to be a full spectrum woman is wonderful, desirable, and possible.

Endnotes

1 Deida (2006)
2 Thomashauer (2002)
3 Thomashauer (2003)
4 Linn (2002)
5 Deida (2006)
6 *Ibid*

CHAPTER TEN

The Warrior and the Man of Wisdom

Ishmael had a pistol he'd traded for a car,
Stolen from the high rise where rich zealots park.
He flashed it at the owner of Acme Tool and Die,
Who drilled him with a shotgun and didn't blink an eye.

~from *Martyr's Wardrobe*~

Theo and his twenty-year-old son Nathan are engaged in weapons practice on their back lawn. They are fencing with shinai (two handed bamboo practice swords), and both are wearing heavy sweatshirts, helmets, and gloves. They first started kenjitsu when Nathan was four, and their practice has changed over the years. As Nathan matured, Theo had to wear more equipment and generate more power to hold his own. Now Nathan is using his superior speed and strength to dominate, while Theo has to rely more on experience and guile to penetrate Nathan's defenses. Finally, after an eighteen-stroke exchange ends with Theo striking Nathan on the wrists, Theo decides to quit while he's ahead:

Theo: "I'm done."

Nathan: "You always decide to stop after you score."

Theo: "What can I say? I'm old and tired."

Nathan: He wipes sweat out of his eyes and feels a glow of satisfaction at how well he fought. "Dad, there's something that's been on my mind."

Theo: Sitting down on the garden bench and looking up with interest. "What's up?"

Nathan: "I'm a junior at college and I still don't know what my deepest purpose is."

Theo: He knew he wanted to be a psychologist at fifteen, and sympathizes with the frustration of yearning for deep soul's purpose without a clear sense of direction. *"The poor guy."* "I know it's hard. You've been doing the right things. You've been taking the classes that attract you, and engaging in the activities that feel most meaningful, but sometimes it takes awhile."

Nathan: "I don't know what to do. I'm graduating next year and I want to keep expanding and growing, but I don't know what direction to go. I don't want to go to graduate school just to go. I want to go with purpose."

Theo: "That's the right attitude."

Nathan: "I feel directionless."

Theo: "It makes me think about what Jade talked about in the desert." Theo and Nathan did a men's retreat three years previously on the Green River in Arizona with their Shaman friend, Jade. The group was three young men and four older men in their fifties, and the focus of the work was embracing the archetypes of warrior and man of wisdom.

Nathan: Smiles, remembering. "Jade said that the young warriors should take lots of risks and the men of wisdom should pass on what they've learned."

Theo: "What makes a warrior, son?"

Nathan: "Someone who does his best to live his principles, and has resolute acceptance of death."

Theo: "What do your principles tell you about your dilemma?"

Nathan: "That I should keep searching and experimenting."

Theo: "Remember to stay fully present in each moment."

Nathan: Looks around at the lush garden on this sunny autumn morning and smiles. "It's a beautiful day."

Theo was introduced to the archetype of the warrior through martial arts, but a warrior can find deep purpose in any endeavor. People with a more masculine essence tend to be happiest when they experience themselves as giving their best gifts, being true to their principles, and having resolute acceptance of death.

Just as in relationships, there can be first stage, second stage, and third stage principles. First stage principles involve doing what it takes to win, and the only rules that matter are the ones you have for yourself. Second stage principles are egalitarian, 50/50, and non-hierarchical as in everyone gets the same treatment, and no one is better or worse than anyone else. Third stage principles involve doing what best opens the moment and serves love.

In 1645, Myamoto Musashi, who for decades had been the preeminent samurai sword fencer in feudal Japan, wrote *A Book of Five Rings*[1] about his understanding of the Way of the Warrior. In it, he asserted that the first thing in the Way of the Warrior was resolute acceptance of death, and offered nine rules for living a life consistent with the Way:

1. Do not think dishonestly.
2. The Way is in training.
3. Become acquainted with every art.
4. Know the Ways of all professions.
5. Distinguish between gain and loss in worldly matters.
6. Develop intuitive judgment and understanding for everything.
7. Perceive those things which cannot be seen.
8. Pay attention even to trifles.
9. Do nothing which is of no use.

These principles reflect a central source of bliss to masculine people, self-discipline. Life may be a burden, but if all intrapersonal/ interpersonal relationships and behaviors are organized by his best understanding of his principles, a man feels a certain indefinable satisfaction of knowing he is being true to his warrior nature.

Musashi was very specific about stance (relaxed and balanced), spiritual orientation (determined though calm, not letting your spirit be too high or too low), timing (feeling into the rise and fall of the moment), gaze (sight and perception, large and broad), and attitude (adjusting to each situation) in meeting adversity.[2] All these skills tend to be satisfying to a masculine person in dealing with the vicissitudes of life and love.

Just as a wide-open, full spectrum woman is in harmony with the Goddess, a man at peace with himself is in harmony with the Warrior. He anchors himself in his deepest consciousness, and then moves to open the world with his presence, humor, shadow, and deepest gifts. Therapy that doesn't acknowledge the masculine's need to experience self as the Warrior misses accessing these essential aspects of masculine existence in service of healing and loving. Theo taught these principles to his children, and also utilizes them daily with his clients.

Man of Wisdom

Often, when a man reaches his fifties, the old standards of victory/defeat, gain/loss, and success/failure are not as absorbing or as interesting as in his earlier life. At this point he's usually yearning to transcend his warrior identity (not leave it, but include it in a larger self) and transition into the Man of Wisdom, what Eric Erickson called the Generativity stage of psychosocial development.[3] The Man of Wisdom hungers less to compete, and more to teach and pass on hard earned life lessons.

Interestingly, this corresponds to a body of developmental research that shows that there is accelerated development on the self-line beginning in the fifties.[4] Theo is in the midst of his own transformation into Man of Wisdom, and still looks somewhat wistfully at his warrior sons as they pit themselves against big waves, formidable opponents on tennis courts or playing fields, social risks, and life struggles.

In the following individual session, Don's identity as a warrior takes center stage as he deals with challenges at work. Often, in the middle stages of therapy (when a working alliance has been established between therapist and client, and the focus of the work has been mutually established and partially realized), clients bring in life problems, or seemingly unsolvable issues, to reconceptualize and work through. These situations all provide opportunities for the therapist to further support the client discovering who he is, to explore where he needs to expand and develop, and to provide challenge and/or support in service of health and growth:

Don: "So the regional manager said that since this guy paid his premium a day after his doctor's appointment, we don't have to cover the surgery. I had told the guy it wouldn't be a problem , and I feel bad for him and his family."

Theo: *"Damn insurance companies. Stop it, Theo! They're necessary and there's lots of good people—like Don here— in the business."* "How are you dealing with it?"

Don: "I just got the call this morning, and I haven't decided. This regional manager is a hard driver, and he's important to my business. On the other hand, it's wrong not to cover this guy."

Theo: He knows that the masculine grows best in the presence of loving challenge, but also that, if he were given the choice between his livelihood and moral ambiguities of this nature, he would also feel conflicted. "This is a tough situation. What are your alternatives?"

Don: "I could just tell the guy the company won't cover him, and that I did all I could, or I could raise hell with the company until they covered him; he's a responsible guy and I told him it was fine."

Theo: Challenging Don to bring his own authority (anchored in his principles) to bear on the situation. "I have no idea what the best legal or business decision is in this situation. It is completely out of my area. But you're an expert in insurance. What's the right thing to do?"

Don: *"The heck with it, he deserves to be covered."* His voice deepens and his face becomes suddenly more resolved and mature. "I told him it was fine, so I'm going to raise hell with the company. I do lots of business with them. If I'm strong I can get him his coverage."

Theo: Feeling a warm admiration for Don. "You're being a warrior."

Don: Liking how this sounds. "What do you mean?"

Theo: "A warrior is someone who does what is right, and resolutely accepts the outcome, even it that outcome is death. A warrior lives by his principles."

Don: Laughing. "This sounds like that karate stuff you talk about."

Theo: Laughing with him. "I certainly learned a lot about the Way of the Warrior from martial arts, but this is more about how you live your life and be true to your masculine essence. It fits in with being present with Nancy, breathing deep, standing straight, looking people in the eye, serving the moment, and getting a hold of yourself when you collapse."

Don: "I was tempted to just let this thing with the guy go. It's going to be a dog fight to get him his coverage."

Theo: "A warrior doesn't seek conflict, but when his principles tell him to put it on the line, he puts it on the line."

Don: Feeling a sense of power in his solar plexus. "Right."

In this exchange, Theo is speaking from his Man of Wisdom, and, using his years of experience and training, is guiding Don to inhabit his Warrior. As Don does this he shifts out of his indecisive defensive state and into a state of healthy response to the present moment. This is reflected by the fact that, rather than becoming more anxious at the prospect of taking on the regional manager, Don is relaxing as he resolves to be true to his principles.

Late that afternoon, Don's having his weekly tennis match with his archrival, Larry, at the municipal tennis courts by the harbor. The courts are situated in a park of green grass and tall, old growth trees, but neither man is paying attention to the beauty that surrounds them. They are absorbed by the life and death struggle on the court. They split the first two sets, and Don is serving for the match at five games to four. Larry is a tenacious opponent who rarely misses late in a match. It's Don's advantage as he steps up to serve. His hands start to sweat. *"Don't choke now."* Don serves a double fault on match point, a classic tennis collapse. Usually under these circumstances Don gets self-critical and flustered. He can see

126

Larry gaining confidence on the other side of the net. This time he remembers his session with Theo and catches himself. *"Relax, breathe deeply, and do your best. The worst that can happen is that you die."* He finds this strangely reassuring, and hits a stinging first serve for a winner. *"Wow. That's great, but relax, don't get too high or too low."* Larry feels the change in energy and rises to the occasion. They battle mightily into a tiebreaker which Larry wins fourteen to twelve.

> Larry: Flushed and excited by the quality of tennis at the end. "Good match, Don. I can't believe the tiebreaker."
>
> Don: Rather than feeling as bad as he usually does when he loses, he feels peaceful. He gave it all he could. "It's amazing what resolute acceptance can do."

Endnotes

---

[1] Musashi (1974)
[2] Ibid
[3] Erikson (1998)
[4] Wilber (2003)

CHAPTER ELEVEN

Trauma

I remember the sea fight far away
How it thundered over the tide
And the dead Captains as they lay
In their graves overlooking the moonlit bay
Where they in battle died
And the voice of the mournful song
Comes over me with a chill
A boy's will is the wind's will
And the thoughts of youth are long, long thoughts

~from *My Lost Youth*, by Henry Wordsworth Longfellow~

It's eight P.M. in Harvey's office and he is in the middle of an intense enactment of childhood trauma with Denise as the central character, and other group members arrayed as stand-ins for her family of origin. Such enactments are useful when clients are sturdy enough to tolerate the stress, and genuine healing is probable because the client seems able to safely identify with traumatized aspects of self (always immature and egocentric to some extent), and can embrace those aspects with clean boundaries and love.[1] Denise has always repressed or denied the damage done to her by neglect and abuse as a child, and tonight she is feeling, owning, and learning how to integrate the terror and outrage she experienced regularly during her formative years. Denise has been going to the group for ten weeks now. She has told the members her story, and has listened to their stories. All members of the group are trauma survivors of some sort. She has supported them in their efforts to heal, and they have supported her. There are three other women and two men in the group. They include:

- ❖ Susan, whose husband left her and their two teen sons for his lab assistant. Her father was a tyrant who bullied and occasionally beat Susan and her siblings. She is playing

Sally, Denise's mother, who chose to ignore her daughter's abuse and attempt to drink her way out of her problems.

❖ Max, who used to spend all his spare time partying and womanizing, which resulted in his wife leaving him. During his divorce, he got into therapy, realized he was wounded, and dedicated himself to healing. His uncle, who molested him regularly starting when Max was five, was discovered to be a pedophile when Max finally confided to his parents at nine, and eventually served six years in prison for molesting Max and several other children. Max is playing Henry, the abusive stepfather.

❖ Felicia, twenty-two, is the baby of the group and tends to play the child when threatened. She was ritually abused by her grandparents as a toddler and young child, entered treatment young, and is psychologically sophisticated for her age. She is playing Denise's alter ego as a child.

❖ Earnest is married to Judy, who suffers from obsessive-compulsive disorder. Judy is in individual therapy with Harvey, and also has conjoint sessions with Harvey and Earnest. Judy was raped as a sixteen-year-old, suffered years of drug abuse and two suicide attempts, and then got onto Paxil and into recovery. She met Earnest in an AA group and married him when she was twenty-five and he was thirty-six. Their marriage has been explosive and emotionally traumatic for Earnest who was raised by conservative, fundamentalist parents in a Jehovah's Witness culture that allowed no deviance from accepted standards, and totally rejected him when he became a hard partying, drug and alcohol dependent college student. His life changed when he entered AA at twenty-seven, and then changed again when he hooked up with Judy. They had a baby daughter who died of SIDS at six months, sending Earnest into a deep depression. They now have a healthy three-year-old son and have been married six years. Earnest is playing Denise's immature, hippy father, Tim.

❖ Alice is thirty with two young kids, is addicted to pot and Vicodin, and is gradually learning how much her addiction screws up her family's life, and how hard it is to change. She recently began attending NA, but still uses episodically. She was the oldest of four children and, after her father left her severely bipolar mother when she was eight, essentially had sole responsible for the safety of her siblings. She is playing Tammy, Denise's younger sister.

Harvey is focused on keeping the process moving and monitoring all the participants for their reactions. He knows that enactments work best when there is a specific purpose and agenda, when each participant can handle the emotional intensity without decompensating into characterological defensive states, and the leader keeps the action progressing forward without bogging down.[2] His clinical goals include encouraging Denise to feel the hurt emotions she has dissociated from throughout her life, supporting transformative moments where new perspectives and aspects of self might be experienced on a visceral level by Denise and other group members (who will all have different associations and restimulations from the enactment), supporting community in the group by organizing them to work together in service of healing, and deepening his diagnostic understanding of group members as they participate. Like all good group leaders, he is simultaneously monitoring the person he's addressing, the rest of the group, and his own inner thoughts, feelings, and impulses as he directs the work. At this point each person has been coached by Denise as to who their character is, and Harvey is beginning to dig in a little deeper, reaching for the feelings and beliefs that Denise has avoided throughout her life:

> Harvey: Directing Denise to address Max who is playing Henry, her abusive stepfather. "Tell Henry how you feel about how he treats you."
>
> Denise: Somewhat timidly. "I don't like it when you touch me."
>
> Felicia: As Denise's alter ego, she has no trouble calling out an abuser. Abuse survivors can be like bloodhounds when detecting abuse. They feel it and want to assert their voice; the voice they didn't have as young children. "That doesn't say it nearly enough. You are a slimy criminal to molest a little girl. You should die or rot in jail forever." Denise, to her surprise, feels a flicker of anger and

131

moral outrage at Henry. *"She's right. What he did was despicable."* Harvey directs Max to respond as Henry.

Max: As Henry he's been coached to downplay and deny. He finds it surprisingly easy. "I never forced you. I always made sure you had a good time. What's the harm? It's just human touch."

Denise: Now genuinely angry. "You'd get drunk and molest a eight-year-old girl. How dare you ask, 'what's the harm?"

Max: He feels a flash of shame and looks away. "I'm sorry."

Harvey: *"She's owning anger at Henry. Stir it up. Get the family involved."* He speaks to Susan who's playing Sally, Denise's mother. "Where were you when all this went down, Sally?"

Susan: As Sally, all she can feel is guilt. "I need a drink."

Felicia: As the young Denise she is enjoying this. The people who ritually abused her were sick beyond any hope of redemption and, since she believes they deserve no compassion, she feels free to indulge impulses to attack Denise's parents. "You drunk loser. You let him molest me for two years, and now you want to dive back into a bottle. Fuck you."

Denise: Starts to cry as she gets how cornered and abandoned she was by her alcoholic mother and abusive stepfather. "I tried to tell you and you wouldn't listen. I needed you."

Susan: As Sally she feels a tired sense of defeat. "I'm sorry. I was just too sick, drunk, and selfish to listen to you."

Denise: She's disgusted with her mother, but also has a fleeting image of the distorted hell her mother' life has been. To the surprise of everybody (including herself) she turns on Earnest playing Tim, her father, and lets him have it. "Mom, at least, had an excuse. She was a drunk. Where were you? You just collapsed after the divorce. I needed you to protect me and Tammy, and you were just weak."

Earnest: Uncomfortable with the role playing, but trying gamely to support the process and be the Tim/father that Denise has described. "Your mother moved and made it hard. I still spent time with you. I still supported you when you refused to go back. You never told me Henry was molesting you."

Denise: Realizing she never did trust her father with the information, and he did support her in her refusal to spend time with her mother and stepfather after ten. She feels some compassion. "I know you loved us. I needed you to notice how unhappy I was, and stand up and fight for us."

Max: "At least it stopped when you were ten."

Alice: As Tammy, Denise's younger sister, she has been withdrawn during the enactment, unconsciously mirroring Tammy's real life childhood defense of being invisible. Suddenly, she can't hold back. "It stopped for Denise, but what about me?"

Denise: Surprised. "You said he never touched you."

Alice: "Yeah, but I was there when he was molesting you. I had to live with them knowing he was hurting you in some mysterious, awful way. I had to listen to their lies."

Felicia: Speaking with the easy cruelty of youth. This enactment has stirred up her capacity for sadism (an energetic legacy of her own abuse), which will be compassionately examined later in group, and individual sessions. "Big deal. They weren't molesting you."

Alice: Crying. "But I was all alone."

Denise: Her natural caring reaching out to sister. "I'm sorry honey. I was too young and too messed up to think about you right away, but you came to live with us real soon. I kept pestering Daddy." Harvey directs Earnest to respond to Tammy.

Earnest: Warming to the role. He is a parent who has lost a child, and his heart reaches out to the two child figures. "I

133

deserted you too, Tammy. I'm sorry, I just always figured you were the stable one."

Harvey: Seeing Denise slump down into her chair as the magnitude of her family's pathology is uncovered. *"Acknowledge and integrate. Get her body involved."* "Denise, sit up straight, breathe deep into your belly, look them in the eyes, and tell your parents what their neglect and abuse has resulted in for you. Gesture with your hands as you talk."

Denise: As she sits up and breathes into her belly, she visibly matures and deepens. Harvey is helping her animate her mature caring aspect to evoke compassion and depth of consciousness. He knows that she needs to feel responsible for self-soothing and growth, and that, for her to discern and trust these qualities in men and other women, she needs to cultivate and inhabit them in herself. She faces her simulated family of origin. "Henry, your sick sexuality taught me that men couldn't be trusted, so I pick untrustworthy men. Mom, your selfish life never showed me how to be a healthy woman, so I had to pull myself up by my own bootstraps, and it's never been easy for me to have intimate woman friends. Dad, you being weak and stoned made you the last person I could trust with explosive information. I've had sick relationships, Tammy's had drug problems, and neither one of us has created a healthy family. I'm going to grow and love and I don't care how screwed up you were or are, or what you did to me, I'm going to love and be happy." Her tears now are coming from her heart, from knowledge of her wounds and certainty that there is a deeper, stronger part of her that feels the wounds, but does not identify with them. The group is silent in appreciation. Harvey senses this is a natural place to stop and let everyone talk about their experience. Much group leadership is first supporting emotionally charged encounters, and then processing them to support intimacy, self-soothing, insight, integration, autonomy, and growth in all members.

Harvey: "OK. Let's share with each other what we just went through, and what it teaches us about love, responsibility, family, and self care."

Over the years, there have been a variety of approaches to dealing with trauma. Desensitization, dramatic reenactment, cognitive restructuring, insight, relationship therapies, and various body therapies including Reichian, neo-Reichian, Pat Ogden's sensorimotor work, and hands on energetic healing have all been used successfully to address trauma. Research by people such as Peter Levine[3], Besel van der Kolk[4], Alan Schore[5], and Susan Johnson[6] has taught us that, although there are always exceptions, optimally resolving trauma can be a complex process that benefits from combinations of healing experiences including:

- Feeling, organizing, directing, and reprogramming physiological reactions.
- Helping the trauma victim integrate non-conscious and conscious memories, and heal relationships with the past (which may or may not include revisiting specific traumatic events).
- Anchoring the work in the individual's physical and emotional strengths.
- Supporting secure attachment styles in current relationships.
- Maintaining a focus on acceptance and liberation of self in the present moment.

Harvey is using the power of the group to help Denise feel the distress she has been resisting conscious awareness of all her life, and to support her discernments that the abusers were ugly, wrong, and sick, and she is both blameless in being the victim of abuse, and yet also responsible to create healing and growth from all her life experiences including the abuse and neglect. He addresses her bodily habits and reactions as he tells her to sit straight, breathe deep, and directly confront her family members. Other aspects of her defensive structures, relational patterns, and current work will be explored with the group as they process their experiences.

This enactment was facilitated by previous group work that built trust and skills in the members for healing trauma. As they continue to process, different group members will discover opportunities for their own deepening and growth. Felicia will have a window into her sadism, Alice will have deeper insight into her power to hurt or help people she loves by participating in life or checking out, Earnest will further clarify the difference between codependence and healthy caring, and so on.

Harvey will continue to direct and balance the work while monitoring all group members, and his own inner experience. As this complex community of interpersonal and intrapersonal relationships rolls forward, guided by loving intent, clear boundaries, and everyone's sense of responsibility to do right, integration, healing and growth will occur in all the members.

It is a central part of Harvey's purpose in life to study, support, and direct such healing. As he often asserts to his clients, the way to resolve trauma is to do what it takes to feel stronger, wiser, and more beautiful as a result of your life experience. Trauma is never a preferable method of growth, but when trauma occurs, growing through it and integrating it into a stronger, wiser self is the way through to love.

Endnotes

[1] Hellinger (2008)
[2] Nichols (2007)
[3] Levine (1976)
[4] van der Kolk (2005)
[5] Schore (2003)
[6] Johnson (2005)

CHAPTER TWELVE

Normal Struggles

A band of lace defines the line
Of thigh and velvet black as night
Your hair backlit in the lantern's light
Black velvet here tonight

Time and again when I was lost to you
Streets all gray, tired up and used
Always must come around and back to you
Black velvet, fell in love with you.

~from *Black Velvet*~

It's six P.M. on a Tuesday evening at Don and Nancy's house. Julia is spending the night with a friend, and Michael is away on a Santa Barbara Middle School trip. The week has been long and stressful, and Don and Nancy are sitting on the back porch drinking wine and talking about their day. It's been four months since therapy started, and they are much closer. The air is brisk, with a faint scent of wood smoke from a neighbor's fireplace, and Don has his arm around Nancy's shoulders. Feeling cozy, Nancy snuggles a little closer and Don kisses her. Loosened up by the wine, she responds with more passion than he's accustomed to, and he suddenly becomes self-conscious:

Nancy: With a seductive smile. "Do you want to step inside?"

Don: A little taken aback. *"She's really hot."* "Sure." They walk into the house and she pulls him down on the couch. He protests. "The kids, what about...?"

Nancy: Caught up in the eroticism of the scene. "The kids are gone. Where's your sense of adventure?" They continue kissing and fondling, and proceed into taking off each other's clothes. Don is simultaneously turned on and distracted as they do this. Unbeknownst to Nancy, this is an eerie reenactment of a hot scene he shared with Denise a year ago in her apartment on Anacapa Street. He discovers that he's lost his erection, and his anxiety increases. Nancy notices. "What's wrong, Don?"

Don: *"I can't tell her what I'm remembering. I don't know what's wrong. I want her. She's ready."* "I don't know. Maybe I'm just tired."

Nancy: Now she's frustrated and hurt. This has never happened with Don. Sex has been progressively more fun since they started doing it again, and she's come to rely on lovemaking happening whenever she wants it. She's not used to being turned on and having Don unable to continue. Reflexively, under the influence of the wine, the frustration, and the unexpected threat, she enters a defensive state and becomes suspicious. Being feminine, she unconsciously feels his weakest spot and leans into it. "Does it have anything to do with her?"

Don: Literally frozen. In the old days this is the kind of information he would effortlessly hide, but he's been working hard on being more open, and so he's caught between the desire to avoid a certain fight, and his developing practice of openness. "I don't know. Not entirely."

Nancy: Now plugged in, disinhibited by the wine, and caught in the old familiar groove. "Well go have sex with her then!" She gets up and storms into the bedroom. Don looks miserably out the window. *"Well, at least we're having a session with Theo tomorrow."*

The next day Theo walks into his waiting room and immediately notices the coolness and tension. *"Something's going on."* He cordially greets them and they quickly get settled and start talking about the previous day's episode. Theo probes a little, and Don reluctantly admits he had a distracting association with an experience with Denise and didn't know what to do:

Nancy: Angry and contemptuous. "What's the point of working on this marriage. He'll never get over her. I thought we were doing so well."

Don: Genuinely sorry for the previous night. He had been having a great time, and feels like he was a jerk for screwing it up. "I'm sorry, Nancy. It's never happened to me before."

Theo: "So, let me get this straight. A hot romantic moment was happening, which is a really good thing. You, Don, were distracted by how turned on Nancy was, had a random guilty association, and lost your erection. You, Nancy, were naturally frustrated and then outraged that Don had a Denise association while you were making love. You stormed off into the bedroom, and you, Don stayed on the couch and watched TV." Both nod their heads. "Then what?" Both looked confused.

Don: "Then I went in after I knew Nancy had gone to sleep."

Nancy: "What do you mean by your question?"

Theo: "A good moment turned into a bad moment, and then it stayed bad. Did either of you consider doing anything about it?"

Don: Interested. "Like what?"

Theo: *"Confront Nancy through him."* "Like what might serve love. Don, what would have both pleased and surprised Nancy?"

Don: "I have no idea."

Nancy: "He'd already blown it."

Theo: "So, love wasn't possible at that moment?"

Nancy: "He couldn't get it up. His penis spoke for him. He obviously didn't want to have sex with me."

Don: "That's not true, I wanted you. I was having a great time."

Nancy: "That's bullshit."

Theo: Laughing. "You both just took 'no' for an answer. Come on. What could you have done to create more love? That's the purpose of your relationship, loving connection."

Nancy: "What can I do? He couldn't get it up."

Theo: "There are a lot of fun, interesting things you can do with an non-erect penis. The only problem is, just when you start getting into one of them, your partner usually gets an erection." A thoughtful look appears on Nancy's face. "I can tell you're getting ideas, Nancy. What do you think stopped you from considering this last night?"

Nancy: "I just got so hurt and angry."

Theo: *"The feminine needs loving praise."* "I think it's so beautiful that you know you're hurt these days, and not just mad."

Don: Still collapsed somewhat. "I don't know what to do when you're so angry." Nancy bristles, and Theo speaks quickly before she dives deeper into the relational defensive pattern.

Theo: *"Masculine needs loving challenge."* "You're collapsing right now, Don. Take a deep breath, soothe yourself, and think about what might serve love when Nancy's angry. What does she need right now? What does she want in her heart when she's so mad?"

Don: Remembering the work he's been doing. "She needs my presence."

Theo: "So what could you have done last night when you lost your erection?"

Don: Smiling. "There are some fun things I can do too when I don't have an erection." This catches Nancy's attention, and she smiles in spite of herself.

Theo: "You two tell me what needs to happen."

Don: "I can pleasure her, if she'll let me."

Nancy: "I don't have to give up so quickly."

Theo: "Absolutely. When you give up on love in the middle of a fight, you lock yourself and your partner into conflict for an extended period. If you soothe yourself and reach for loving contact, all kinds of good things are possible.

This is especially important to remember when you've been drinking. Alcohol can make you more interested in sex, but less able; especially when you're a guy and you're tired. You agree it was a hellacious week." They both nod. "So, this was a great time until it blew up. You, Nancy, couldn't stand it that Don wasn't on the same wavelength as you, so, rather than reach through your frustration and anger to get him on the same wavelength, you fell into the old pattern. You, Don, saw Nancy coming into her sexual power and didn't know quite what to do with her. Rather than relax and learn how to enjoy her new sexiness, you collapsed into anxiety and self-absorption."

Don: "Now what?"

Theo: *"Loving challenge."* "You tell me."

Don: Smiles at Nancy. "Hey baby, want to go out tonight?"

Nancy: Laughing. "Julia did ask if she could spend another night at Cindy's house."

All couples struggle regularly with their intrapersonal and interpersonal relationships. What characterizes healthy couples and individuals is not whether they have struggles, but how they deal with themselves and each other when issues inevitably appear. Deal with struggle better, and problems with love get less frequent and less severe. Deal with struggle worse, and problems with love get more frequent and more severe. These are the normal rhythms, the normal struggles, of relationship.

CHAPTER THIRTEEN

Transference and Countertransference

Moments we are hovering,
then fall from grace recovering.
Sure could use another drink.
No, maybe not another drink.
Moments we are hovering,
then fall from grace recovering.
Before you leave this consciousness,
be sure to feel my greatest gift.

Here it is,
here it is I love it, yeah.
O baby,
when you sing me the rain song.

~from *Rain Song*~

Denise is talking to her therapy group six weeks after the enactment session where she began to re-own, reprocess, and reprogram her identifications, bodily memories, and associations with her chaotic childhood. She's been feeling much better, and looking great. Denise has always liked healthy food and exercise, but now she's taken both to new levels and, as many people do when they're adjusting to being single, she showing the benefits of her new regimes in increased radiance:

Denise: "This guy at the office asked me out, and I'm tempted."

Susan: "Isn't this the guy who has a lover?"

Denise: "He's been seeing this woman in San Francisco for a year and a half and it's not going anywhere."

Felicia: Groans. "Not another guy in a relationship."

Denise: "He says they're about to break up."

Max: "That's what I used to say when I was cheating on my wife."

Denise: Defensive now, she feels under attack. "He's a sweet guy. All he did was ask me to coffee."

Harvey: Addressing the group. "It sounds like some of you are concerned and angry at Denise for considering going out with another guy who's in a relationship." There's general ascent. "What do you make of this, Denise?"

Denise: "I don't know. I'm confused. What, I shouldn't go out with anyone unless he's perfect?" There is an angry murmur in the group, and Susan (whose husband cheated and left) bursts out. "Don't you get it? Men are dogs. What about the woman in San Francisco? Do you think he's telling her he's interested in you?" Denise is taken aback by this. She has learned to not deeply consider the feelings of other women in these dramas.

Harvey: "Everybody breathe deep and feel the violence in the room. Where is it coming from in each of us? There's patterns here of interlocking defensive states. Feel your feelings, but discern the patterns, especially your parts."

Susan: "My part is to say nothing and then feel ripped off when people do damage. I pretended to trust my husband when he said he had to work late and have business trips, but I knew something was wrong. Sure, I'm mad, but I'm also speaking up for you, Denise, and for that woman in San Francisco. This is the same problem of secret relationships that can only end in a big mess." There are nods of agreement.

Denise: Clearer now that the group is processing the patterns rather than attacking her. "You're right, but I'm so lonely. I guess I should tell him 'no.'"

Harvey: "What's your pattern Denise?"

Denise: "A nice man is sweet to me, and I like the attention. I like how I feel when someone like that wants me. I guess I hope it will work out better each time."

Harvey: "You tell us what's the healthy thing to do."

Denise: "To only go out with men with integrity." She turns to Harvey and smiles brilliantly. "Men like you, Harvey." The group laughs and kids Harvey mercilessly for thirty seconds.

Harvey: Feeling a rush of distracting pleasure at Denise's attention, and a wave of powerful sexual polarity between them. He is suddenly aware how desirable she is. He knows that this extra charge is both transference in that Denise is projecting an idealized masculine figure onto him, and countertransference in that he's responding by projecting an idealized erotically radiant feminine figure onto her. Attraction between feminine Denise and masculine Harvey is a natural consequence of energetic polarity, but transference involves extra charge. This extra, distracting intensity is the projection of archetypal positive or negative figures (in this case, positive) onto another. Harvey being single (and somewhat lonely in his personal life), and Denise having a pattern of attracting unavailable men adds even more intensity. Harvey is aware of this and immediately adjusts the polarity from his side to be more appropriate, and resolves to consult with a colleague about his countertransference. He also perceives that the pattern they all are discussing is happening right now. Denise and he are energetically constellating an inappropriate relationship. *"Too much pleasure, talk to Janet about it later. Right now, work with it."* Denise, you seem to feel drawn to me at this moment."

Denise: Uncomfortable with being so explicit. "No, I just think I should choose men with integrity."

Felicia: "That's such bullshit. You're fully coming onto him."

Denise: Indignantly. "I am not!"

Harvey: "I'm sure you're not consciously coming on to me Denise, but when you smiled at me and said, 'Men like you,' I felt a wave of feminine erotic radiance pour in my direction. You have a lot of it. I needed to take a deep breath and focus." He turns to the group. "Did anyone

145

else feel it?" Everyone nods and agrees. "Max, Earnest, what did you feel?"

Earnest: Very uncomfortable. "I don't know."

Max: "I felt attracted to Denise."

Denise: "I'm not coming onto Harvey!"

Harvey: "It's not that you're consciously coming on to anybody, or that feminine erotic radiance is bad. It's a wonderful thing. Some people's defenses make them more invisible when they're threatened." "Like me." Interjects Alice, and everyone laughs because they had, indeed, all stopped being aware of her as things got conflicted. "Some people get more radiant when threatened. That's one of your defenses, Denise. And feminine radiance always magnetizes attention and erotic polarity. Also, you tend to offer devotional love to men you trust in the present moment, like me, while unconsciously avoiding evaluating whether they are appropriate candidates for relationship."

Denise: "I do think you're a good role model for a man."

Harvey: "Sure, I'm a trustable man, but, as your therapist, am I a good role model for a relationship? Wouldn't both of us have to violate all kinds of boundaries to have even a social relationship? When else in your life have you been in this situation?"

Denise: Getting it. "I see it now, especially with Don. He was married and my boss." Again radiating extraordinary erotic light, and speaking with an innocent, seductive tone. "But, if it's unconscious, what can I do?" This time the group laughs more compassionately. They get it that she's generating this energy out of her awareness.

Susan: The vulnerability associated with such eroticism is more than she can stand. "Men will say anything to get laid. They'll lie and cheat. Trusting them is just setting yourself up to get screwed in more ways than one." More laughter, but some uncomfortable glances from Max and Earnest.

Harvey: "Do you really believe that there are no trustable men, Susan?"

Susan: Beginning to cry. "Sometimes I wonder."

Enjoyable attractions and distracting attractions.

It's ten AM the next morning and Harvey is on the phone with Janet, a psychologist friend with whom he consults regularly. After the group last night he called and left a message with her because he was concerned about the intensity of his desire for Denise. It was a distracting attraction. The difference between enjoyable attractions and distracting attractions is significant. Enjoyable attractions are those erotic hits that naturally take place throughout social existence. Enjoyable attractions tend to be validating to everyone involved. Distracting attractions are attractions that distress or irritate. They linger and can contribute to both intrusive pleasurable fantasies of sexually charged relating with the object of the distracting attraction, and/or intrusive unpleasant thoughts about other love interests where there is perceived deprivation (often perceived erotic deprivation in an ongoing lover relationship). A classic example of this latter phenomenon is a man having a distracting attraction to another woman and later picking a fight with his wife. Harvey isn't currently in a relationship, and so his sense of erotic deprivation is more general and not focused on a specific person as it would be if he had an erotically unfulfilling marriage, but the intrusive distracting attraction is focused on Denise.

Positive/negative transference/countertransference.

Positive transference is when there are charged pleasurable feelings a client has for a therapist that are based in the client projecting idealized figures onto a therapist, with accompanying feelings of love, attraction, and/or desire for closeness and special relationships. Denise demonstrated this when she revealed how she was idealizing Harvey as a symbol for a good man.

Negative transference is when a client experiences charged painful feelings and critical beliefs that arise from projecting demonized figures onto a therapist, with accompanying loss of empathy, and the presence of hurt, anger, fear, and/or frustration leading to violent impulses to self flagellate, attack others, or run away.

Positive and negative countertransference involve a therapist experiencing extra-charged pleasurable or painful feelings for a client that are based on the therapist's projections. Harvey can discern that his distracting attraction towards Denise is a form of positive countertransference, and he is asking Janet's help to work through it so he can be clearer and more impeccable in his therapeutic relationship with Denise. Talking to an understanding and trusting confidant is often enough to transform distracting attractions into enjoyable attractions. Further, countertransference feelings, when appropriately processed, help the therapist have deeper consciousness and more compassion in helping a particular client:

> Harvey: "So she said, 'Men of integrity, men like you Harvey', and I felt this huge rush of desire. For a moment it was really disorienting."
>
> Janet: She knows that Harvey's boundaries are superb, and that he is no threat whatsoever to be sexually inappropriate with a client. She also knows that he has often been lonely since years before his divorce, and that he found it difficult to separate from his last lover. "What attracted you, Harvey?"
>
> Harvey: "She was just so beautiful, vulnerable, and feminine."
>
> Janet: "But there seems to be an ache, an extra boost. What is that about?"
>
> Harvey: He has a sudden image of himself, his ex-wife, Cherise, and their three-year-old son twenty years ago on a beach in Big Sur. Cherise was wearing a green bikini that used to drive him crazy with desire, and they were all so happy on that trip. "I just thought of me and Cherise on a family trip to Carmel back in the eighties. Those were good years."
>
> Janet: "You sound sad."

Harvey: *"I am sad."* "I liked it when Jeb was little. I though Cherise and I would be together forever."

Janet: "Is Denise like Cherise?"

Harvey: *"God, I loved Cherise in that green bikini."* "They are both erotically radiant. They are both wounded. I always wanted to take care of Cherise, and I feel more investment than I should in Denise not repeating her same pattern."

Janet: Confronting. "What is it with you and beautiful, wounded, emotionally vulnerable women?"

Harvey: Thinking slowly in this defended area, he reaches for deeper perspectives. "I feel powerful and secure when they need me to take care of them."

Janet: *"Focus on his wounds and responsibilities."* "What's a healthy relationship for you?"

Harvey: *"OK, it's making sense now."* He unconsciously sits up straighter in his chair, and focuses his gaze out the window as he talks. "I think it scares me to consider being with a woman who's self-validating, mature, and erotically radiant. The feminine was not safe for me in my family of origin. You've met my parents."

Janet: Remembering Harvey's passive father and immature, dominating mother. "I could see a few engulfment issues coming out of that system." They both laugh.

Harvey: "I think I've got it now. I block out Denise's immaturity when she shines that erotic light on me. I'm not feeling the distraction at this moment. I'm feeling more compassion like I do for all my women clients."

Janet: *"Take the next step, Harvey."* "And?"

Harvey: Suddenly confused. "Whoa, I just blanked out."

Janet: What's the message for you in this? There is some personal work here that you need to do."

Harvey: Feeling lonely, and correctly interpreting what that means to him. *"You've been avoiding match.com. You chickenshit."* "I need to use my abilities to discern mature radiant women and take the risk of approaching and affiliating with them. I've been chickening out."

Janet: She hears the self-critical attack. "That's not the most self-supportive tone I've heard this week." They both laugh again.

Harvey: "It's so easy to forget that violence towards self blocks risk taking and growth. I want romantic love so much, and yet it gives the woman such power to hurt me. I guess that's one of the reasons I go for wounded women who seem to need me to stay balanced."

Janet: "We both know where that goes."

Harvey: Smiling. "Yeah, straight to hell."

At the next group meeting, Harvey finds Denise attractive, but not distractingly so. This makes it easier for him to set clear energetic boundaries for Denise who, without being consciously aware of the process, turns down her defensive erotic radiance in response to him being a truly safe man; one who's integrity will not collapse in the face of her feminine test.

Negative transference and negative countertransference operate out of the same psychological structures as positive transference and positive countertransference (projecting past material onto another person), but, at first glance, look very different. The following is from a session Mary and Julie had later that week. Mary's been on three-week vacation in Japan, so this is their first session in over a month:

Mary: *"She looks so tired."* What do you want to talk about today?"

Julie: Yawns deeply. *"Don't tell her."* "I don't know."

Mary: "You seem so tired."

Julie: *"Shit, she notices. Don't tell her."* She uses a defensive tone. "I'm fine."

Mary: *"Something's going on."* "What's the deal, Julie? It feels like you're hiding something."

Julie: *"Tell her."* "You're just going to tell my parents."

Mary: *"Oh oh. Sex or drugs."* "Look, I try to keep as much private as possible, but I have to do something if I feel somebody, especially you, is in danger."

Julie: *"She'll tell them for sure. Forget it."* She speaks angrily. "Never mind then."

Mary: Laughing now. "Right. So, how do you like the weather this week? Pretty sunny, huh?"

Julie: Laughing back. Wanting to discuss what's on her mind. *"Tell her."* "OK, well, me and Heather have been smoking meth."

Mary: She feels a shiver go up her spine and a feeling of dread in her solar plexus. *"God, I hate that stuff. Don't get distracted, open her up."* She carefully uses a neutral, interested voice. "When did you start?"

Julie: "About four weeks ago."

Mary: *"Probably partly some transference, she didn't want me to leave and didn't schedule any individual sessions with Theo like I suggested."* "Right around our last session?"

Julie: Seeing no possible connection. "Yeah, I guess."

Mary: "How often are you smoking it?"

Julie: "Every day. We go home and smoke, and last week, we smoked before school a few times."

Mary: Appalled at how frequent the use is. *"She might be addicted right now. It can get you fast. You are way too upset about this. Put the countertransference on the back burner. Keep opening her."* "How does it feel?"

Julie: "I like it. I don't like smoking pot anymore. I like meth better."

Mary: "What do you like about it?"

Julie: Yawning again, without irony. "I feel good and energized when I smoke it. I'm still doing fine at school."

Mary: "How often last week did you smoke it more than once?"

Julie: "About five times."

Mary: "How often more than three times?"

Julie: "About four times."

Mary: "So, a majority of the days you are staying high all day. Did you smoke it today?"

Julie: Genuinely offended. "I wouldn't smoke it before our session."

Mary: *"Gently now, this is an opening."* "Why not?"

Julie: Puzzled for some reason. "I don't know, it just seems wrong."

Mary: "So, according to your current values, it's not right to smoke meth before therapy, but it's OK at school, at home, or with your friends?"

Julie: Uncomfortable. "Yeah."

Mary: "Are you worried at all?"

Julie: *"Wow. I am worried."* "I guess. I know it's bad for me. And when it's, you know, a time I have a chance to smoke, I really want it. I don't know if I could not do it if I had it."

Mary: "How is it bad for you?"

Julie: "Well, I have trouble sleeping. I have to lie about it to my family, and that sucks because my mom and I were getting along better and things at home have been happier. I have to hide it at school and from the kids who don't smoke. I can feel it pumping my body up when I do it. I'm sure that's not good for you. And I just think about it so much now."

Mary: "What do you want to do about it?"

Julie: *"I wish I could stop."* She's surprised at the thought. "I'd like to stop."

Mary: "Can you?"

Julie: Uncomfortable. *"Maybe not."* She wants to look strong for Mary, though. "Sure, any time."

Mary: "It's a bad sign when someone who uses daily is that confident they can stop. Usually it's much harder than you think, and you need much more support than you realize. Do you really think you can just stop?"

Julie: Feeling flash of panic. *"I don't know if I can."* "I'm worried that I can't." She has a sudden image of her mother in hysterics. "You won't tell my parents?"

Mary: "I think you should."

Julie: Suddenly furious. "No way! I knew you'd do this. I knew you'd tell them. Well, I'm not! I won't! My mom is just like you. She'll disapprove and go crazy."

Mary: Feeling defensive and worried. *"Slow it down, Mary."* She relaxes into her chair. "So, your mom is just like me, and you think I'm disapproving and going crazy right now?"

Julie: "It's crazy to even suggest talking to them about it, and I'm not going to." She jumps up and literally runs out of the session.

Mary spends several minutes centering and meditating. She's acutely aware of rushes of worry, resentment, and frustration. She can feel her heart pounding, and she keeps reflexively replaying the session to see if she made any errors, and to prove to herself that Julie would have exploded no matter what she did. She notices this and smiles ruefully, recognizing the negative countertransference. Julie's drug use and accusations have combined to form a narcissistic wound that has penetrated Mary's customary equanimity and resilience. She decides to call Theo and ask for support and advice in taking the next step in dealing with the problem. She has signed releases from everybody to talk to Theo, but mainly she calls because she knows that he's a solid support source who will get Julie talking about her meth use, and who will help the family with the issue. The following exchange is just after she finishes telling him the story:

Theo: "I've been most worried about Julie all along. There's a certain capacity for angry recklessness in her that scares me. So, how are you feeling as you tell me about it?"

Mary: "Better. I'm beginning to get the countertransference under control. I think I've been unconsciously seeing her as a reflection of what a good therapist I am. She's really made phenomenal progress. It's hard to see her crash like

153

this. I don't feel like such a brilliant therapist right now."
Both laugh.

Theo: "How do you think we should deal with it?"

Mary: "Well, she's safe physically. They're not shooting up, and clearly they've got dosage under control. I'm inclined to give her a week to talk herself into telling her parents. If not, then I can insist in the next session. If she comes to the next session."

Theo: "She values your relationship. She'll be back. I think you're right, she's mad now because you've been magical, and yet you can't magically save her from this struggle. Her negative transference is the let down of that primitive idealization."

Mary: "Don't get all psychoanalytic on me now, Theo."

Theo: Laughing. "If the shoe fits..."

Mary: Laughing. "OK, OK, I'm Cinderella. What are you going to do?"

Theo: "I've got another family session scheduled in a week. I'll wait until Julie talks to them (or you inform them), and then we'll deal with it in that session."

Mary: "Sounds good. Thanks for the support. This one got to me."

Theo: Remembering similar experiences over the years. *"Transference and countertransference come with the territory."* "You've done the same for me, Mary, more than once."

Harvey and Mary are doing what most good therapists do when they encounter transference and countertransference issues; they are seeking support and direction from a community of colleagues to transform transference and countertransference into healing work with their clients and themselves. Other people can often see and feel our patterns better than we can. Therapists who ask for and receive such support do better in every way.

CHAPTER FOURTEEN

Parenting

You remember every date,
I know you write them down, I still appreciate.
Send a card or gift that's great.
Don't you know you are so cool?
And it makes you beautiful.

When old lovers kiss you cry,
Salty happiness, always feels so nice.
When things get dangerous you're strong,
Like that pool in Istanbul
And it makes you beautiful.

You tend the garden for us all
And it makes us beautiful.

~from *You*~

Theo walks down the stairs into the kitchen on Saturday morning. The sink is full of dishes and ants have found a little piece of chicken than his daughter, Chloe, has left out. It's her job to do the dishes each night, but she got in late from a movie last night at ten, and apparently felt entitled to eat a snack and leave the kitchen dirty. Muttering darkly to himself, Theo starts cleaning the kitchen. Sandy walks in, happy with the day and looking forward to spending the morning gardening. She sees Theo cleaning and muttering:

Sandy: *"Oh no. He's mad Chloe didn't clean the kitchen."* She tries to good-vibe him. She was raised to be a balancer, placator, and accommodator, and she hates it when he creates conflict. "Thanks for doing the dishes."
Theo: Crabby. "Ants are all over the place because a little piece of chicken was mysteriously left out. I can see

why ants are thirteen percent of the world's biomass. Somebody didn't clean the kitchen."

Sandy: *"I hate it when he rants about Chloe."* She tries to normalize the situation. "They find the tiniest piece."

Theo: Sarcastically. "I guess it just slipped Chloe's attention."

Sandy: *There he goes."* "Yuck."

Theo: *"Lighten up you dope, Sandy hates it when you rag on Chloe."* He smiles at his Prussian disgust with his daughter's cleaning habits, and reminds himself for the thousandth time that he was worse at sixteen, that Chloe has gotten progressively better at self-care, self-soothing, and being considerate, and that her personality restimulates the primitive, conditioned rage he learned fighting with his mother throughout his development. *"What if she were smoking meth like Julie? Don and Nancy must be sick with worry. Chloe works hard on herself, and thank God she does."* "I'm sorry. I'll be nice to her and politely remind her to, please, clean the kitchen after she snacks at night."

Sandy: Smiles back. "That's better." At that moment Chloe comes clumping down the stairs. She is not a morning person.

Theo: "Good morning sweetheart. How'd you sleep?"

Chloe: "Pretty well."

Theo: "You know, when you leave little bits of chicken out, the ants come."

Chloe: "OK. It was just so late and I was too tired."

Theo: *"She never just says, 'I'm sorry, I'll do better.' She always gives an excuse."* He notices himself slipping into a defensive state. *"Stop it! You're picking a fight right now. Use a warm tone."* "Well, maybe next time you could do a quick chicken-check before you go to sleep." "Chicken-check" gets both Sandy and Chloe laughing. Theo notices the warm vibe and congratulates himself. *"Good job, Theo."*

This interchange reflects decades of work that Theo, Sandy, and Chloe have cumulatively done to make their family work better. When the children were small, Theo would often indulge his angry impulses to lecture sarcastically (or to just check out and work on his projects), and Sandy would routinely suppress and tolerate her repulsion at his collapse and try to counterbalance with niceness and/or exhausted accommodation. Chloe learned to just ignore Theo when he was hostile, and Sandy subtly encouraged her to do so by not setting her own boundaries when Chloe was angry and aggressive. Over the years everybody grew. Theo became much more self-soothing and self-regulating when angry, and realized he needed to participate more supportively in the emotional life of the family at all levels. Sandy learned to discern when it served love to set boundaries for the kids and Theo, and cultivated the openness of showing Theo her "yum" and "yuck", and directing, even frustrating the kids when it was necessary for their development. Chloe and her brothers gradually developed more insight, responsibility, and care, and learned that respectful confrontation was honored in their family, but nastiness and disrespect evoked consequences.

Our responsibilities as parents.

At the center of all this work is Theo and Sandy embracing their core responsibilities of parents; the responsibilities to be true to their own paths, to create and maintain secure, joyful passionate intimacy with each other, and to maintain a shared vision of their family as a community whose purpose is to support everybody's health and development. Over the years they worked on parenting their own immature or wounded selves. Theo learned to parent his hurt/angry inner child who wanted to attack uncaring attitudes. He cultivated capacities to hold onto that child, contain him, and teach him how to better serve love. Sandy gradually got better at doing the same for the child in her that tended to dissociate, passive-aggressively collapse, or avoid all the pleasures and joys of the world.

At an attachment and trauma conference I attended in Irvine California, John Gottman, arguable one of the preeminent couples researchers in the world, made a series of startling observations about parenting. He pointed out that "99%" of parenting books were written on how to control children, and that what research indicated children needed most were parents that were accessible and responsive 30% of the time. "Three hundred is a good batting average in the major leagues, and it's a good batting average for parents" he asserted to an appreciative crowd of students, Marriage Family Therapists, and Psychologists.[1]

At the same conference, he also reported research indicating that secure attachment relationships with mothers were not the be all and end all of parenting. A father's participation in family life and child rearing had huge positive influences on everybody's well being in the family.

What makes all these wonderful parenting activities challenging so much of the time? Sound parenting principles are relatively obvious, and more people in our culture are aware of good parenting skills than at any other time in U.S. history. The reasons why parenting is so often difficult are the subtle but powerful influences of defensive states, and the complexities and demands of development.

Intergenerational transmission of defensive states

In the above example, Theo felt the pull to reenact historic conflicts he learned as a child. His family of origin, especially his mother, fought freely, and often attacked sadistically, verbally and physically. When stressed in certain ways, Theo feels amplified anger and contempt, distorted beliefs about others being selfish and uncaring, and strong impulses to attack. These are the defenses that were imprinted on his body and nervous system as a child, and will always be present in him to some extent.

Chloe was born the same physical and emotional type as Theo's mother. Research has demonstrated a variety of traits to be present to varying degrees in different combinations at birth including novelty seeking, harm avoidance, dependence, self-directedness, self-transcendence, persistence, and cooperativeness[2]. Chloe is intelligent, powerful, anxious, sensitive, and aggressive, and, when distressed, her attitudes and behaviors easily cue Theo's defensive systems. To the extent he has cultivated compassion and depth of consciousness, and to the extent he receives confrontation and direction from the environment (especially Sandy), Theo can be aware of defensive states, soothe himself, and be caring and non-alarmed in the face of Chloe's defensive acting out. She'll be egocentric, aggressive, non-empathetic, or unthinking in her defensive states, and, like many children and teenagers, will tune Theo out if he responds angrily or contemptuously. He's learned that patience and compassion are his challenges in parenting his daughter.

Sandy, on the other hand, grew up in a family where explicit conflict was forbidden to everybody. When stressed in certain ways, Sandy feels blank, has self-critical beliefs about her worth as a woman and a mother, and has impulses to accommodate, balance, and smooth over rough edges. When Chloe was a toddler, rather than set limits, Sandy would keep giving until she often collapsed physically or emotionally, leading to numerous fights with Theo who felt attacked and deserted by Sandy's exhaustion and suffering.

In the interests of growing and doing right, Sandy cultivated compassion and depth of consciousness, and learned that, to the extent that she receives confrontation and direction from the environment (especially from Theo), she can be aware of defensive states, feel her feelings, soothe herself, give clear feedback (her "yuck" to Theo is a great example), and set clean limits in service of love. She's learned that setting consistent, firm boundaries in service of her personal comfort and Chloe's development are her main challenges in parenting.

Defensive states and structures are natural outgrowths of normal development. Good parents cultivate awareness and responsibility for their defensive states. Attending to their relationships with their distressed, immature inner aspects—their inner children—is a great technique for accomplishing this[3], and helps them guide their actual children to learn how to do the same. Parents thus teach by example, and by being accessible and responsive. They provide love and limits. When the kid needs a hug, you hug her.

When she needs a time out, you give her the time out. When she needs encouragement, you encourage, and when she needs to be frustrated, you frustrate appropriately with mature compassion. Contrary to the early *Summerhill*⁴ dreamers—who idealistically thought children would always self-regulate if given space and permission—life without boundaries is less likely to create altruism and transcendence in children, and more likely to create entitlement and narcissism.

Developmental lines and levels, children are not little adults.

As we discussed in Chapter Five, we are born egocentric, almost entirely undifferentiated from our physical environment. Under the influences of our drives to create meaning, affiliate with others, establish position on subjectively important social hierarchies, and to be true to our deepest masculine and feminine essences, we grow. We discover our physical body as separate from the universe, our emotional selves as separate from our parents, and our conceptual capacities as first having magical powers over the universe, and then, when we discover we can't directly control the environment through force of will, we find we can indirectly control it through asking or coercing our parents to use their Godlike powers.

Between four and seven we begin to develop increasingly urgent needs to follow the rules and be accepted into our primary community of family, and then nested communities of school, spiritual assembly, city, state, nation, and, ultimately, the world. Along the way to adulthood we naturally grow from more self-centered to more other centered, from more cognitively primitive and concrete, to more cognitively complex and multi-conceptual. Our needs can mature from "I want what I want when I want it," to "I want to belong to, and be accepted by, important groups," to "I want to successfully compete in merit based hierarchies," to "I want everybody to have the same care and rights, and screw anyone who disagrees with me," to "I see the beauty, good, and truth in all points of view, and I need to serve deep soul's purpose and/or love."⁵

As more masculine types we develop to be attracted to feminine shape and energy, to want rights first for ourselves and then for everybody[6], to hunger to know and claim a feminine partner, and to delight in deepest consciousness and deep soul's purpose.[7]

As more feminine types we develop to be attracted to integrity and presence, to want care first for ourselves and then for everybody[8], to hunger to be known and claimed by a trustable masculine partner, to be nourished by pleasure in the body, and to delight in being an open channel of emotion and a wellspring of love.[9]

Development is a messy process where we glop and slop back and forth on many developmental lines. A reasonable conversation with a five year old can be followed instantaneously by a temper tantrum. A professor can lecture from deepest understanding of his topic, go home and, feeling threatened seeing his wife being friendly with the postman, turn into a suspicious, needy toddler, desperate for external validation. An eight-year-old can find an abandoned baby bird and have a moment of extreme altruism, caring for all living beings, and then hit his brother with no thought of the suffering he's causing. A judge can evaluate and rule on complex, arcane law, and come home to happily have a tea party with her grandchildren.

We can have peak or regressed experiences at any moment as we move three steps forward, two steps back, and one step to the side on various developmental lines. On the other hand, stable development on every line, the point where we naturally feel most at home when we're relaxed and open, proceeds in levels; levels that include and transcend each other as we grow. We are not born caring and become selfish. We are born selfish and become caring. We are not born with formal operational cognitive skills, and then grow to think in primitive, magical fashion. We are born with immature cognitive skills and then grow to understand Aristotelian either/or logic, and then broaden the scope of our intellectual powers to hold competing concepts simultaneously, and use our imagination to inhabit an astonishing array of "what if?" scenarios.

Being accessible and responsive to a child means meeting that child in his or her current worldview, which is not necessarily the same as our current worldview. Supporting development is not demanding that our children skip levels as they grow; it is identifying the levels that they are in, supporting them expanding into those levels, and then guiding them toward developmental shifts to new abilities and perspectives.[10]

Not understanding that children often have different worldviews than adults, and that children often think differently than adults, can lead to astounding misperceptions. If a father tells a nine-year-old that he will kill him if he ever smokes cigarettes again, that child might actually believe his father is capable of physically killing him. A two-year-old who is being abused by a child-care worker probably assumes that parents know what's going on, because parents know everything. Knowing the universes our children inhabit, and speaking to them in languages that are comprehensible in those universes is central to being accessible and responsive.

We don't skip levels.

Understanding that we don't skip developmental levels provides valuable insight and direction in parenting. A four-year-old is only marginally aware of the nuances of right and wrong. Often what is moral to him is what he can get away with, and lectures on altruism and ethics leave him frustrated and confused. I advise parents with four-year-olds to compassionately and firmly teach them the rules of engaging the world. "It's the rule that, if we have two cookies, you get one and your sister gets one." "It's against the rules to lie." "The rule is, when I tell you to get into the car, you get right into the car." Six to eleven year olds identify strongly with their families, and are motivated to follow the rules and occupy the roles that help them feel securely embedded in those family cultures, and securely attached to family members. Eleven to fourteen year olds, coming into their cognitive abilities to hold competing concepts simultaneously in their consciousness, and hungry for unique adult identities, can look for deeper, more personal principles of right and wrong, and often shift their conformist tendencies outward from their families to more emphasis on peer groups, and cultural icons.

Since teens have sophisticated moral structures in place, I advise parents to ask their teens what their values are, and then to encourage their children to honor their own developing ethical and aesthetic systems.

The self-line and the specific abilities lines.

There are a number of developmental lines divided into two broad categories of self-line (including the cognitive, moral, psychosocial, psychosexual, and values lines), and the specific abilities lines (mathematical, musical, kinesthetic, and artistic are examples). People can be deep on one line and shallow on another.[11] In *The Right Stuff* Tom Wolf's premise that, "The right stuff is not transferable," reflects his own take on this crucial fact, discovered by observing test pilots' often held belief that, since they were gifted pilots, they were gifted in everything, with disastrous results[12]. More significantly to parenting, children tend to learn at different rates on different lines. A child who learns to read at four might take till ten to be able to effectively throw a baseball. Parents who don't understand this run the risk of expecting too much of their children in areas of difficulty, or missing children's unique gifts in areas of natural strengths—for instance, a child who struggles in school, but who grows to be a professional race car driver, artist, or rock musician.

Each child develops uniquely in this multidimensional developmental framework. Growth is very much call and response between children and parents. An aggressive child needs firm external boundaries and guidance towards learning healthy internal self-regulation. A shy child needs support in affiliation and appropriate risk taking. An intellectually hungry child needs enrichment, stimulation, and cognitive challenge. All children need love and boundaries from parents who are accessible and responsive at least 30% of the time.[13]

Parents tend to parent their children the way they parent themselves.

An organizing principle of parenting is that you tend to parent your children as well or as badly as you parent yourself. If you meet your personal shadow sides with compassion, humor, and the intent to serve love, then you are more likely to meet the conflicted sides of your children with compassion, humor, and the intent to serve love. If you appreciate, enjoy, and liberate distressed and repressed aspects of yourself, you can more fully support and liberate distressed and repressed aspects of your children. This interplay between a parent's interior relationships with themselves and their family relationships is of crucial importance to the health of families.

The following is the family therapy session the week after Julie told Mary about smoking meth. As Theo predicted, Julie told her parents about the drug use the day before the session. Rather than enact their historic pattern of fighting with each other when things were going badly, Nancy and Don called Theo, oscillating between concern and panic. Nancy was frantic on the phone, and Don wanted to leave Michael home to "protect" him from the distress. Theo soothed Nancy, and weighed in with Don that Michael—who at this point was the least distressed family member—almost certainly already knew, and that it would be better for everyone, including him, if he had a chance to participate in dealing with the issues and helping out. So far in the session, Julie and Nancy have described how Julie told Nancy she was smoking meth, and Theo has progressed through the same series of questions that Mary did in her session, tracking the history, scope, and possible ramifications of Julie's methamphetamine use:

> Theo: Noticing Michael fidgeting. "What's your reaction to all this, Michael?"
>
> Michael: "I think it's messed up. I don't like how upset everybody is. Julie doesn't seem worried about using drugs. It's like, she doesn't think it's wrong, or dangerous, or anything."

Julie: "I want to stop, but it's hard cause a lot of my friends smoke meth, and all of them smoke pot and drink."

Nancy: "I'm so sick of your loser friends. I should tell all their mothers what they're doing."

Julie: Horrified at this potentially catastrophic embarrassment. "You can't do that, Mom. No way!"

Nancy: "You have no idea what you're doing to us."

Don: Uncomfortable with Nancy's hostile tone, but sick with worry for his daughter. "Your mother's right, this is too dangerous."

Julie: "I knew I shouldn't have told you."

Theo: *"Except for Michael, they're all avoiding the real issue."* "Julie, how do you want this to turn out?"

Julie: *"I'm so tired of my life."* "I want to stop using meth, and I want my parents to leave my friends alone."

Theo: "Don't you have friends who are in recovery? You know, who stopped using drugs or alcohol and go to AA or NA meetings?"

Julie: "My friend Sherri stopped smoking meth last May and has been going to teen NA meetings."

Theo: "Do you think she'd take you to some meetings?"

Julie: To her family's surprise. "She already offered when I talked to her yesterday. I told her I would."

Don: "That's great sweetheart."

Nancy: "I think you need a hospital. A program like in that movie, twenty-eight days."

Julie: Getting scared now. "I don't want to be hospitalized."

Theo: Teaching. "You do what it takes to save your life, but I think it's good to go in stages, especially under the circumstances. Even though all the signs point to addiction, you've only been using regularly for a couple of months, you have good family support, and you seem motivated to change. Are you willing to start going to NA meetings, Julie?"

Julie: "Yes."

Nancy: "How will we know? She's been lying for years now about one thing or another."

Julie: Falling back into the easy groove of fighting with Nancy. "Great, just keep calling me a liar. That really helps."

Don: Triangulating with Julie against Nancy. "Don't bitch at her, Nancy."

Nancy: Sarcastically. "So, I'm a bitch now? I suppose I made her use drugs?"

Theo: "It's easier to fight than to face the problem, isn't it?" Nancy, Don, and Julie become silent. "Julie, I also want you to go see Dr. Janice Ledbetter to be evaluated for antidepressants. She's a psychiatrist I know who's great with teenagers. Often people who abuse drugs or alcohol are unconsciously self-medicating anxiety or depression. One of the atypical antidepressants, buproprion, has also recently shown promise in reducing craving for methamphetamine."

Julie: Without irony. "I don't need drugs!" Theo shrugs, smiles, says, "OK," and looks with raised eyebrows at Julie. She gets it, and starts to laugh and is quickly joined by Don, Nancy, and Michael. "OK, OK. I get it. I'll go see her."

Theo: "The principle for your parents, Julie, is to provide whatever support is necessary to protect you life and nourish your growth. Therapy has really helped your sense of self, and your ability to relate with your family, but substance abuse and addiction often needs more support than just psychotherapy. Your meth use became out of control fast, which suggests you are particularly vulnerable to this form of addiction. Maybe NA meetings and medication, plus all the good stuff you've been doing the last six months, will create a recovery program that will adequately support your health and development. I think you have a capacity for addiction. Many studies show that there are genetic predispositions to various forms of compulsivity, but, whether it is biochemical vulnerability or something that you've developed through your life experience, you have a current addiction to deal with. I'm worried about you smoking meth, but seven weeks of regular use is not the same as three years of regular use. The more central question is, 'How long have you been using drugs and alcohol to change your mood?"

Julie: "I first started drinking and smoking pot when I was thirteen."

Theo: "And how do you feel when you can't get high for some reason?"

Julie: "OK sometimes. Sometimes I wonder if it's worth it to be alive." There is a horrified silence following this revelation.

Theo: Notices Michael staring out the window. "Tell your family what you're thinking, Michael."

Michael: "I think that too sometimes." This shocks Don and Nancy. Michael is the well-adjusted, happy one in the family.

Nancy: Flowing into her denial system. "No you don't. You've always been a happy child."

Theo: "Maybe Michael believes that's what you need from him. To always appear happy. Michael, how do you deal with it, when life doesn't seem worth living?"

Michael: "Watch TV, play video games, or hang out with my friends."

Nancy: Yearning out to love her son. "You should talk to us. We could help."

Michael: "You get upset when I'm unhappy. It's better if you think I'm happy all the time."

Nancy: Defensive. "Parents get upset when their children are unhappy. It's natural. We can handle it. Just trust us to deal with stuff."

Don: "Yes, you can tell us. We can handle it." Now Julie and Michael look at each other and start to laugh.

Theo: Looks over at Don and Nancy. "What do you make of this?"

Don: "I guess the kids haven't had much success talking to us."

Nancy: "If you weren't off with that woman, maybe you'd have been more help to all of us." Don's lips tighten in anger, Michael looks away, and Julie rolls her eyes and groans. Nancy looks defiantly at everybody.

Theo: *"Can they take it up another level?"* "Don, what's valid about what Nancy just said?"

Don: He's suddenly confused. He's grown accustomed to Theo getting Nancy to back off when she attacks him about Denise. He's also embarrassed talking about his affair in front of the children. On the other hand, he trusts Theo, and so he does his best to answer the question. "I should have insisted that Nancy and I get into therapy instead of going off and having an affair. I was keeping secrets of my own. No wonder my kids keep secrets." The family looks on respectfully. This is powerful truth coming from husband and father.

Theo: "How about you, Nancy? What have you done to create a closed system?"

Nancy: Don's integrity is pulling her to be more loving. She reaches for her responsibilities in closing people down. "Me getting so mad and being so bossy probably didn't help people relax and share. I was quicker to complain than to insist we find ways to love each other better. Also, Michael just said he feels sad, even suicidal, sometimes, and I disagreed with him about his own feelings." Julie especially is impressed with this. She's just not used to her mother acknowledging her part of problems. She feels strangely protective of her mother all of a sudden.

Julie: "You've been much easier to talk to since this summer, Mom." Michael nods his head. "Julie's right."

Nancy: Tears form in her eyes. "Well, thanks. I've been trying hard."

Don: Feeling protective and proud. "You've done a good job working on our relationship Nancy."

Theo: *"Time to consolidate."* "OK. First, Julie, I suggest
  you follow through with Shari to take you to some NA
  meetings. I think daily meetings would be optimal
  for at least the next two weeks, and, if Shari can't go,
  I recommend Nancy and Don go if the meetings are
  open meetings. At the meetings, look for a woman who
  you really like and respect. You might want to ask her
  to be a sponsor." Everybody nods. "I'll give you Dr. Sally
  Ledbetter's number, and Don, Nancy, and Julie can go
  talk to her about possible medications."

Don: "What if all this doesn't work?"

Theo: Talking to the whole family while answering Don.
  "Parenting is always about making adjustments. If your
  kids are thriving, keep doing what you're doing. If they
  have problems, work with them to make adjustments
  to solve the problems and create more health and love.
  The adjustments you make for a three year-old are
  different for the adjustments you make for a thirteen-
  year-old, unless." He pauses and looks meaningfully
  at the kids, "Unless your thirteen-year-old is acting
  like a three-year-old." The kids laugh, but they get the
  message. "If meetings and therapy don't work to help
  Julie keep abstinent from drugs and alcohol, there is out-
  patient care, residential programs, and hospitalization if
  necessary. It's like climbing a ladder.

Julie: "That stuff won't be necessary."

Theo: "I admire how you and your family are dealing with
  this, Julie. You're probably right, but if not, so what? You'll
  probably be a parent some day, and experience it for
  yourself. The principle is, you do what it takes to create a
  healthy, joyful life for yourself and your family."

Do what it takes to create a healthy, joyful life for yourself
and your family. As Don and Nancy are discovering, for each
parent this begins with attending to your own personal health
and development (taking responsibility for all your intrapersonal
and interpersonal relationships), and proceeds into doing what it
takes to make love work with your spouse. Married partners need

to support each other in being able to provide a non-alarmed, supportive presence for children in the context of being accessible and responsive. We all need help in doing this. Often this help comes from other family members, friends, books, groups, school, spiritual assemblies, and/or psychotherapy. One of the beauties of modern American life is that, for those with the courage to ask, help is always available.

Endnotes

[1] Gottman (2005)
[2] Cloniger (2004)
[3] Witt (2007)
[4] Neil (1969)
[5] Wilber (2000)
[6] Gilligan (1993)
[7] Deida (2006)
[8] Gilligan (1993)
[9] Deida (2006)
[10] Witt (2007)
[11] Wilber(2003)
[12] Wolfe (1979)
[13] Gottman (2003)

CHAPTER FIFTEEN

Transitions

Ethan is leaving childhood
Waving goodbye to friends and family
His room is filled with memories, pictures of his family
Trophies, toys, and books are mostly left behind.

When a boy becomes a man,
He tries so hard to understand
A woman's plan and childhood dreams keep haunting him.

When a boy becomes a man,
He finds it hard to stand the pain
Of losing love and finding strength to love again.

~from *Leaving Childhood*~

It is Saturday, three months after the Julie meth-smoking session, and Don is at Blockbuster trying to find a video the whole family will enjoy (not an easy task). Julie has been sober, going to meetings, and on an antidepressant for eleven weeks. Don and Nancy have continued to improve, and the talks around the dinner table have gotten pretty psychologically sophisticated. Michael has discovered he has a talent for observing relational patterns, and has been exercising this talent with enthusiasm, which puts a considerable strain on Nancy's defensive habit of trying to control how everybody thinks and speaks. As Don rounds the end of an aisle of the drama section, he comes face to face with Denise:

Don: Shocked. *"She looks good."* "Hey, Denise. How are you?"

Denise: With sensitivity and some sadness. *"He looks content."* "Hi Don. I'm fine."

Don: Struggling. *"What can I say? I'm sorry I hurt her."* "Really? I've hoped that you're doing well."

Denise: *"He's so sweet."* She notices herself beginning the old trance talk that leads her into being seductive. *"Stop that, girl."* "I like my new job, and that therapist you recommended has helped me a lot. I feel happier and healthier than I think I've ever felt before."

Don: He is glad to hear the truth in her words, but feels a pang of loss for when this beautiful woman used to want him more than anything. "I'm glad to hear it."

Denise: Curious about his life. In spite of her better judgment, she asks. "How is your family?"

Don: Feeling shy, and reluctant to talk about his family with her. *"Come on, she deserves an answer."* "Things are much better with Nancy and the kids. Therapy has helped."

Denise: Now she feels a sense of loss. *"But I do want him to be happy."* "I'm glad for you. I'm trying to learn how to have healthier relationships."

Don: He immediately feels defensive and then realizes what he's doing. *"Good for her. She deserves a good relationship."* He smiles. "I guess that's what we're all doing." He adds impulsively, "I'm sorry about everything. I know it was hard for you."

Denise: "It was both of us making mistakes. I think it's turning out for the best."

Don: *"Now what?"* "Uh..."

Denise: Smiling to herself. She knows he gets tongue tied in situations like this and decides to bail him out. "I've got to go. You take care, Don."

Don: "You too, Denise."

Change doesn't happen all at once. In the presence of different stimuli, we'll often shift from one worldview to another, or from one level to another on different developmental lines. We'll enter regressed states either appropriately in healthy responses to the present moment (as in many forms of adult play), or destructively in defensive reactions. We'll have transcendent moments of altruistic care, or post-formal operational intuitive insight (as in peak experiences of deep spirituality), or be operating from an egocentric perspective when we believe we are being mature (as when a boss humiliates a subordinate "for his own good").

Even when we work hard on own development, we often don't notice change and growth, sometimes even when we're put into stressful situations and discover ourselves thinking, feeling, and acting differently. This is what just happened to Denise and Don in Blockbuster. Both were genuinely caring for the other person and related people in their life, and both wanted to behave in a way that served the highest good. Neither considered becoming reinvolved. This felt natural (even ordinary) to each of them, but reflected dramatically different worldviews from the more egocentric ones they were occupying a year earlier.

What's tricky about development is that, given the right cues, old defenses can reappear and lead to distressed, distorted perspectives where progress can be trivialized, and people can angrily declare defeat even in the presence of true victories over reactive destructive tendencies. This is what happens in the following exchange when Don returns home from Blockbuster.

Don walks into the house at 7:00 PM and waves hello to Michael shooting baskets through a hoop they have on their driveway.

> Michael: "Let's play one on one."
>
> Don: He's been obsessing about telling Nancy the details of his encounter with Denise all the way home from the video store. He promised he would tell her if he had contact with Denise, and he wants to be a man of his word. He has been enjoying Nancy more than he can remember and is frightened of upsetting what feels like a delicate balance by bringing a Denise story into the picture. *"I'd love to play, but I've got to get this over with."* "I'd love to son, but I have to go talk to your mother for a while." Michael hears a familiar distress in his Dad's voice, and unconsciously withdraws into practicing three pointers. "Sure Dad." Don walks into the house and sees Nancy sweeping the back porch.
>
> Nancy: "What'd you get?"

Don: "Shakespeare in Love. When in doubt, go for the classics."

Nancy: Laughs. "Good choice, I love that movie." She notices he is nervous. "What's wrong?"

Don: Amazed as always at how feminine people can read energy. *"How does she know, just like that? Spit it out, Don."* "I saw Denise at Blockbuster." Nancy's face clouds up, and Don irrationally feels like he's done something wrong. He unconsciously falls into his old defensive habits of closure.

Nancy: Her familiar, suspicious defensive state is immediately evoked. *"Not Denise again. What happened? Did he know she'd be there? Does he want her? We've been so happy recently."* She waits ten or fifteen seconds for him to go on, but he doesn't. She begins to get angry. "So what happened?"

Slowly over the next thirty minutes she drags the whole exchange with Denise out of him. Under the threat of Nancy's anger, Don has become his old, dense, passive-aggressive self, and so his successful conversation with Denise sounds more and more like an episode of infidelity:

Nancy: Crying angry tears. "So, she looked great, it was good to see her, you talked about us, and you wished her well. I suppose you wanted to have sex with her too?"

Don: Feeling weak and miserable, but actually holding onto himself better than ever before in such an argument. "I told you, yes, she looked good and I want her to do well. She's a good person. I don't want to have a secret thing with her, or anybody else. I won't do that anymore."

Nancy: She hates hearing anything positive about Denise, but she is drawn to Don's integrity as he keeps hanging in to work through the argument. She struggles to not attack him. *"Theo said my real power is my yearning."* "I just want us to be through this thing. I wish I could just see her on the street, or hear about you running into her, and not get so upset."

Don: Moved by her vulnerability. *"Reassure her and comfort her. She can't help getting mad about Denise."* "It'll happen, sweetheart. We all just have to keep doing our best. I choose you. I want you. I love you." Nancy cries more deeply now, less from anger and more from release. Don puts his arms around her and holds her. The rest of the night is spent in different variations of restimulations, attack, heart to heart talk, and comfort. Finally, at 11:00, Don offers direction. "I think we've talked enough for tonight. Let me hold you and we'll go to sleep. We have a session tomorrow. We can work it out there."

Nancy: Trusting him, feeling secure that he's trying to do what's best for everybody. "OK, I'd like you to hold me. I love you, Don." They go to sleep.

The next day Don and Nancy enter their conjoint session with some trepidation. They both feel they had a major setback the previous night, and wonder if they've actually been making the progress that they've thought. They tell Theo the sequence of events, ending with Don suggesting they hold each other and go to sleep.

Nancy: "It's so discouraging. I felt just the same as I did before."

Don: "Yeah, me to. I blanked out, had trouble telling Nancy the truth, and I still have this intense reaction when I see Denise. It's not that I want her, or want to leave Nancy, it's just a big emotional charge to even see her."

Theo: "How did you feel when you woke up?" Don and Nancy look at each other and smile with a little embarrassment. "Oh, so you woke up and made love?"

Don: "It seemed like a better idea than talking more about what happened."

Nancy: "It sure was. I was dreading even coming to the session today. I hate feeling those feelings."

Theo: "It sounds like you resolved the episode pretty darn well."

Nancy: "What do you mean? We were arguing all evening and got exhausted."

Don: "It was a miserable time."

Theo: "Look how many things were different than from a year ago. Don, you knew your purpose and principles when you ran into Denise. You did your best to serve the highest good, and then disengaged as cleanly as possible. In spite of the impulse to hide the encounter from Nancy, you told her, knowing that was the right thing to do. You, Nancy, initially got stuck in your toxic, angry distrust, but turned to your real strength, your yearning for love and truth. When Don offered the best direction he could to help the situation, loving contact and sleep, you correctly interpreted it as him offering depth of consciousness, and responded with devotional love. Don, in the morning, instead of getting hooked into endless second stage negotiation, you initiated love making, and Nancy responded enthusiastically. You two did phenomenally better than before in similar situations."

Nancy: Reassured, but still alarmed at the toxic power of the relational defensive patterns. "But it hurt so much, and was so exhausting."

Don: "Yeah, I'm still wasted."

Theo: "Of course. It took you four hours to get back to love. Keep practicing. Make it shorter next time, and notice it was shorter. Compliment each other for doing it more efficiently. Eventually, if you can hold onto yourselves and create a third stage experience, it could take four minutes. Then it becomes hugely less risky to have restimulations. You're only risking four minutes of pain instead of four hours of stressful effort."

Don: "It really was different. I could tell Nancy was working hard to not attack me. She kept interrupting herself when she did it."

Nancy: "And Don was good. He didn't take off, close down, or get sarcastic like he used to."

Theo: *"They just don't get how beautiful they are at this moment."* "You guys are so beautiful right now, I can't stand it." Both Don and Nancy laugh.

Depth of consciousness is having deep understanding based on appreciating multiple perspectives. Compassion is reaching for the least violent, most caring, and most accurate embrace of individuals and experiences. These qualities often do not come naturally, especially when defensive states are involved.

I occasionally explain to my clients that psychotherapy is in some ways like martial arts training. Anybody can look good executing techniques by themselves on the practice floor, or in carefully executed choreography under the watchful eye of the instructor. The real test is when there is an opponent in front of you in a novel situation. Then everything feels awkward and sloppy, but—if you struggle to do right according to the principles and practices you've trained in—the outcome is often the subjective experience of courage and victory.

Defensive reflexes never leave us entirely. This is a good thing. We learned our defenses when they were the best alternative our nervous systems could come up with in response to dangerous threats. Nancy's rage would be an asset if she were ever attacked in a dark alley. Don's passive-aggressive shut down could keep him out of jail if a particularly nasty cop pulled him over for speeding. What growth gives us is the depth of consciousness to bring conscious attention and disidentification to bear on what's happening, and the compassion to choose love and caring over egocentric manipulation and violence. Sometimes we have to struggle for hours, days, or weeks, with amplified or numbed emotions, distorted perceptions and thoughts, and destructive impulses, before we can break through to caring appropriately for ourselves and others. The effort is always worth it. Five percent of positive effect while trying to do right in the grip of a defensive state is better than a hundred percent of negative effect while surrendering to defensive perspectives and impulses.

Don and Nancy are transitioning from their previous first/second stage relationship to a new second/third stage relationship.

Where egocentric attack was once the standard under stress, and quid pro quo negotiation the best they could occasionally do to address the absence of love and the presence of emotional violence, they now have clear communication as their reflexive response under stress, and third stage giving their best gifts of love to each other as the standard they are both reaching for. This is so new for them that they don't fully comprehend the huge developmental shift it represents for them and their family. They are in transition, consolidating their new gains, and reaching for new perspectives—creating expanded worldviews—that help them understand these new experiences.

Abraham Maslow devoted the last part of his career to studying transcendence. He observed how people grow into adulthood operating from lack, what he called "deficiency needs." We fear there is not enough food, shelter, security, strokes, or resources, and so we want more.

Some of us, as we arrange our lives to feel like there are enough resources available, discover that we are moved to act and give from fullness. We feel so full of love, purpose, and wisdom that we want to give it back to spouse, family, congregation, community, or humanity. Maslow called needs that arise from fullness "being needs."[1] As we attend to our inner and outer relationships, resolve conflicts, and create integration and harmony, we are more motivated by being needs, and less by deficiency needs. We grow from first stage "What's in it for me?" to second stage "Let's talk about it and make it fair," to third stage hunger to give our best gifts of love to each other and the world. When a couple does this on all the channels of their intrapersonal and interpersonal relationships (emotional, erotic, familial, intellectual, professional, spiritual, physical, and cultural) they naturally serve each other in a shared spiritual practice of using their relationships as transformative vehicles of development, service, and transcendence.

Flash forward: five years later Don and Nancy are making love.

It's nine P.M. and they are draped over each other in their candlelit bedroom. The walls are red and there is a huge print of a famous nude by Ingres—called La Grande Odalisque—on the wall. Nancy subtly shifts into the more masculine position of being on top, her legs between Don's, and pumps her pelvis with a possessive gleam in her eye. She occasionally prefers the masculine pole of erotic polarity, and Don enjoys her in it immensely. In tune with Nancy, Don relaxes into the feminine role of expressing pleasure through the body, smiling, moaning, and moving with enjoyment. She starts happily laughing during her second orgasm, and it is too much for him, and he releases, looking as deeply into her eyes as he can. Time and ecstasy stretch out in all directions as they slowly relax into each other's arms. Finally, Nancy starts to giggle.

> Don: Startled out of a reverie. "What?"
>
> Nancy: "We never used to be able to do this."
>
> Don: Laughing. "It seems so easy sometimes, but I know it's not."
>
> Nancy: "Thanks to you, buster."
>
> Don: "Thanks to you." He looks away, momentarily distracted by a memory of painful fighting years ago. "It used to be so hard."
>
> Nancy: Rolls over and tickles him mercilessly. "Come back."
>
> Don: "OK, OK, I just had a flashback." He rolls towards her, smiles, and says teasingly. "I need to focus on you, because it's all about you, baby."
>
> Nancy: Luxuriating in his attention, relaxing fully into feminine pleasure through the body, and surrendering to devotional love and playful connection with Don, who finds her deliciously cute when she's like this. "It's all about me!"

Since development is include and transcend, we can operate from any developmental level we've ever been. Immature states aren't inherently any better or worse than mature states. The relevant variable is what serves the highest good in the moment. Don and Nancy are playing with each other, moving from more serious to more playful, more mature to less mature as the moment dictates. Since they are wide open and attuned to each other, the result is fun, passionate, and loving.

Both Don and Nancy now embrace their masculine/feminine aspects and their deepest sexual essences, and have practiced opening themselves and each other to serve the moment. Nancy, as the more feminine partner, more often brings light, life, warmth, and an open channel of emotion to their life and sexual occasions. Don, as the more masculine partner, more often brings presence, depth of consciousness, relationship with shadow, and direction to their life and sexual occasions. This combination deepens their erotic polarity, and strengthens the love affair that is at the heart of their family.

Suddenly there's a knock on their bedroom door. Don groans and puts a pillow over his head. Nancy pulls it off and pushes him out of bed. "Go see what your son wants." He gets up and starts pulling on clothes and calls out, laughing. "I'm coming, Michael. I've got to get dressed."

Endnotes

[1] Maslow (1962)

CHAPTER SIXTEEN

Transformations

Here we sing,
sitting round a fire.
Some of us are young and some are old.
I was just a babe,
first in such company.
Family never ends it just
flows on...

These are days of joy,
Sun cascading down.
We will keep the old songs alive
In the autumn time.

~from *Days of Joy*~

Don and Nancy have done well in the eight weeks following the video store argument, and they and Theo have agreed to have sessions twice a month instead of weekly. Occasionally in one of the off weeks, Don or Nancy will ask for an individual session. The following session is an individual session that Don has requested.

Even though things are going well, Don is longing for something; but can't seem to put his finger on what it is. Driving to the session he thinks, *"I'm satisfied, no I'm stoked, by what's happening with Nancy. The kids are so much fun now. Michael is going to kick my ass in basketball before he knows it. Work is fresher too. What is it that's bothering me?"* The following exchange is right after he has described all this to Theo:

Theo: *"Feels like spiritual hunger."* "When do you experience a sense of the sacred, Don, a sense of being part of something larger and deeper than yourself?"

Don: "Sometimes when Nancy and I are, you know, really warm, or when the kids surprise me with something beautiful like Julie cooking dinner, or something funny, like Michael spitting up milk on me when he was laughing so hard watching *Blazing Saddles.*"

Theo: "Are there any prayer or meditation practices you've done that involve a sense of the sacred, a sense that you were so full that you were overflowing with love, or meaning, or even emptiness?"

Don: "You mean, like at a wedding or a funeral, or something like that?" Theo nods. "Occasionally, when I'm in the Sierras camping and fishing, it's like I'm part of the river or mountains. Sometimes I feel nature is a huge being, and I'm part of her."

Theo: *"Here we are. Nature mysticism, deity mysticism."* "You notice you call nature, 'her?'" Don looks surprised. "Some say that our deepest unchanging consciousness is our masculine core, and that everything else, especially nature, is the feminine[1]. When you feel one with nature, it's a spiritual practice called nature mysticism.[2] Like most spiritual practices, it's really good for you."

Don: Feeling a deep longing. "There's something that gets to me about this."

Theo: Hearing the yearning in Don's voice. "What are you hungering for?"

Don: "I don't know."

Theo: "If you had your choice of meditating in stillness until you felt one with everything that is arising in the present moment, or of having a communal ceremony with music, movement, people together, food, and family, which one would you choose?"

Don: Without hesitation. "The first one. It sounds more like me."

Theo: "There are two major forms of spiritual practice. One, often called 'the ascending,' is moving away from your physical body towards oneness with pure spirit.

The other, often called 'the descending' is moving into sensation, body, relationship, and nature towards oneness with everything that is arising. Oneness with nature is nature mysticism, oneness with some sense of a sentient God, like the huge being you feel in the Sierras, is deity mysticism, and feeling like you're expanding infinitely into pure spirit, or emptiness, is causal, or formless, mysticism. Most spiritual practitioners have also had moments of non-dual awareness, where there is only one experience that always is, always has been, and always will be.[3] Which sounds most attractive to you?"

Don: "I like the nature mysticism one when I'm camping. If I had to choose one to do at home, the emptiness one sounds best."

Theo: *"He's such a masculine guy."* "Why's that?"

Don: "I don't know. The idea of being one with emptiness just sounds relaxing to me."

Theo: "Would you like to learn a short meditation? It might answer some of the longing you've been feeling." Don nods, interested.

Theo: "All right, let's do it now. I'll put in a fresh tape so you can cue it up easier at home. Relax with your feet flat on the floor and your hands in your lap." Don complies, a little uneasily, but game. "Now, close your eyes almost all the way; just so there is a line of light at the bottom of your vision. Do the circular breathing that I showed you and Nancy in our second session. Breathe in down the front of your body all the way through your genitals, and breathe out up your back through the top of your head." Theo observes Don relaxing and breathing deep into his abdomen. "That's good. Feel your breath go in and out of your body." Theo waits four breaths, centering himself into witness meditation, feeling the path and leading Don deeper down into it. "Feel how you have a body, but you are not your body, you are a deeper witness that observes and feels your bodily sensations, but is not that body or those sensations." Theo feels into Don as he talks to

183

him, waits about thirty seconds until Don seems to be in balance, and then continues. "Now, feel your emotions. They come, they go, and they are pleasurable or painful. Feel how you have emotions, but are not any emotion, you are a deeper witness that observes emotion but does not identify with it, just as you have a body, but are not your body." Don relaxes more easily this time. He's getting into an altered state of deep relaxation and witness contemplation. Again, Theo feels into Don and, when he seems relaxed and in balance, continues. "Now, observe your thoughts and judgments as they arise, come, and go. You have thoughts and judgments, but you are not your thoughts and judgments. You are a deeper witness that observes body, emotion, thought, and judgment, but identifies with none of them. Relax into that witness. Abide as that witness that observes all objects but is itself not an object." Don is now visibly in a meditative state. He is relaxed, focused, breathing deeply, and generating the contemplative aura that Theo has learned to associate with such experiences. Theo opens himself up more deeply to the ocean of consciousness that we all share, and keeping his eyes and attention on Don, meditates with him for about five minutes, focusing on energetic support of Don's practice. "Now, staying connected to what you've been experiencing, when you feel ready, slowly open your eyes." After about a minute, Don opens his eyes and looks at Theo.

Theo: "What was it like?"

Don: "It was like there was a big space, and I was floating in it, and then I was the space."

Theo: "How do you feel?"

Don: "I feel great. Refreshed, like I just woke up from a deep sleep."

Theo: "Ken Wilber in his CD series, *Kosmic Consciousness*, says the witness is our deepest self, always present, and connected to, even one with, the ocean of consciousness that we all share. He says that many spiritual traditions maintain that the ever present witness who observes all objects, but is itself not an object, is who we are in deep, dreamless, sleep."[4]

Don: "It felt like different energy, like I was different sizes. I like the meditation. What should I do with it?"

Theo: "Relax into this ten or fifteen minutes every day. A half hour to an hour would be better, but it's preferable to do it daily for a shorter period than more rarely for a longer period. Use the tape if it's easier or more fun. I like to meditate in the morning before breakfast and after exercise, but you might like it some other time. Lots of research shows that practices such as these lead to enhanced health and faster development[5]."

Don: "Sounds good."

The practice Theo taught Don is similar to many ascending meditative techniques. Ascending techniques tend to be more attractive to masculine types (or the masculine aspect of feminine types). These practices are more solitary, and involve subjective oneness with emptiness, hunger for freedom, and disidentification with gross reality and the physical body. Disidentification is not dissociation. Dissociation involves cutting ourselves off from awareness of what we're dissociating from such as perceptions, thoughts, memories, sensations, judgments, or emotions. Disidentification involves having perceptions, thoughts, memories, sensations, judgments, or emotions, but not identifying with them. Instead, we are identifying with a deeper self that is larger than the experience; a deeper self that observes perceptions, thoughts, memories, sensations, judgments, and emotions as objects, but is itself not an object.

Descending techniques tend to be more attractive to feminine types (or the feminine aspect of masculine types). They involve dance, movement, community, and bodily pleasure in service of devotional love to spirit. While the masculine craves freedom, the feminine yearns for love. Nancy's yoga classes, which she enjoys and attends religiously, are a good example of descending spirituality. They are done communally with other women in a beautiful room, with incense, flowers, and music. Her yoga classes all involve pleasure in the body, relaxation, and intense, mostly enjoyable postures and movement.

Theo knows that spiritual practice supports health and development. If either Don or Nancy was a member of a spiritual community, he would help them find the contemplative aspects of that tradition that most resonated with their subjective sense of the sacred. For instance, if Don was Catholic, centering prayer as taught by Father Thomas Keating might be something he would enjoy. If he were Baptist, daily prayers of gratitude and surrender to God's will might be pleasurable. If Don was a pure rationalist, Theo might frame the practices as biofeedback that has been proven to be beneficial in lowering blood pressure, slowing pulse, and balancing the endocrine system. Whatever a person's orientation, spiritual practice of some sort usually serves health and development.

Don returns home from the session in a contemplative frame of mind. That night at dinner, he tells the family about his experience. None of them notice how wildly different this conversation is from what they all used to talk about (or not talk about) a year ago:

Nancy: "I always feel so good after yoga."

Julie: "I never know exactly what they mean when they say that NA is a spiritual program."

Don: "Don't you have to surrender to a 'greater power?'"

Julie: Bristling a little. "We don't *have* to do anything. We choose to ask a power greater than ourselves to help us."

Don: "What does it feel like?"

Julie: Looking inward, and staring out the window. "It's hard to say. I feel connected to everyone in the room. I feel peaceful. I don't think it's a God or anything, but it sounds a little like what you felt today."

Michael: "Sometimes when I'm surfing, I feel like I'm part of the ocean."

Don: "Theo says that's nature mysticism, oneness with nature."

Michael: "Surfers call it 'stoke.'" Everyone laughs.

Nancy: "I feel it right now with our family.

Endnotes

[1] Deida (2006)
[2] Wilber (2003)
[3] Ibid
[4] Ibid
[5] Alexander (1990), Siegel (2007)

CHAPTER SEVENTEEN

Spiritual Awakening

Some pray to Mohammed or Bahaullah.
Is the wind through the forest your voice of God?
Some meditate in silence and some dance and sing,
Maybe every one of us is everything.

You might think we're different, but we're all the same.
We don't want war, and we don't like pain.
Live for the children, help them see,
We're here to live our own lives, and help others be.

We've got to
Learn to live together,
one people, one world.
Learn to live together,
we know that we should.
Learn to live together,
one people one world.
Learn to live together,
or surely we'll
Never get to heaven with violence and hate.
Yeah, we're here to live our own lives and help others be.

~from *One World*~

Denise at the Calvary Chapel.

It's an overcast, rainy spring Sunday morning, and Denise is singing *We rest in you, our Lord* with the choir at the Calvary Chapel. She has been attending services more regularly since her break-up with Don, and finds the services soothing and uplifting. Reverend Cooper begins a sermon on surrender to Jesus. As he speaks about accepting Christ into your heart, Denise feels a huge upwelling of love and care rising through her. She finds herself praying fervently in a classic born again experience, *"I feel you, Lord.*

I surrender to You. Help me do Your will on earth." Overflowing with love and spirit, she afterwards describes the experience to Reverend Cooper:

> Denise: "It was like a thousand voices all singing at once, and I felt a sacred presence in me and all of us. I feel like a different person."
>
> Reverend Cooper: Confident in his beliefs and his ministry. "It was Christ's spirit you felt. You are born again into Christ, and will never be the same." This makes perfect sense to Denise. Deity mysticism is her most comfortable and natural spiritual experience.
>
> Denise: "What do I do?"
>
> Reverend Cooper: Secure in his faith. "Pray to God each day to be a instrument of His will on earth. Surrender each moment to Christ's love."

Reverend Cooper is echoing a sacred Hindu text, the Bhagavad-Gita, in which the God Krishna, speaking to the warrior Arjuna about karma yoga, advises Arjuna to make everything he does an expression of God.[1] Deity mysticism involves the felt sense of a larger, wiser, more loving presence than is humanly possible, and surrendering to that presence.

Sandy and Theo at home.

Sandy is on the phone, finishing a class with her spiritual teacher, Djwal Khul. DK is channeled through her friend Terri in Sedona, and has been Sandy's teacher for ten years. The class ends with a guided meditation. Sandy relaxes into it, feeling the comforting presence of DK and the other members of the group in various parts of the world.

> DK: "Let pink orange light from the tenth ray wash through your body, filling your aura with energy. Feel your heart chakra expand in a pink bubble around the world, and out into the Three-Star-One, and beyond into the infinite. Offer this light as a gift and a blessing on all sentient beings, so that they may be free from suffering, feel happiness, and experience oneness with all."

As Sandy relaxes into the meditation she hears Theo walk up through the front door from work. He sees her on the couch with the phone headset on and, knowing she's finishing her class, quietly smiles and walks into another room. It is a sweet, secure moment, one of thousands such moments that happy couples share over the course of their lives together. During the thirty-five years of their relationship, Theo and Sandy have had progressively more such moments, and progressively less where they surrender to hurting each other. It looks simple, but is the result of many years of work and practice.

The reciprocal learning of intimates working on themselves and serving each other open is the shared spiritual practice that is accessible to all lovers. It is one of the few spiritual practices that involves relating intimately with another. Shared spiritual practice can be as simple as a brief exchange of caring glances, or as elaborate as an extensive lovemaking ritual in which candles, incense, music, role playing, intense focus, or ceremony are integrated into deepening connection and ecstatic union that shines out from the couple to all beings.

Later that evening Theo is sipping a beer and gazing out at a magnificent sunset over the Santa Barbara Channel. It's a blustery early spring evening. Theo puts on a heavy shirt, steps out on his balcony, and climbs up a ladder to his flat roof, three stories off the ground. Theo's house is on a ridge in the foothills, and there is a panoramic view from the roof. The sunset is a red line against the ocean to the west. The chilly wind blows into Theo's face, and he has to lower his center of gravity to compensate. He walks over to the highest part of his roof. The harbor is down on the left, and the Santa Ynez mountains rise up behind him, the rock faces pink in the sunset.

As the light fades, the Channel Islands are highlighted in the clear air. Theo focuses on opening to spirit with the intent to serve," *I offer this practice to all beings, so they may be free from suffering and achieve enlightenment."*

He stands relaxed, facing the ocean, feet shoulder width apart, and slowly begins one of the Hachi Dan Kin breathing exercises, breathing in deeply down his front through his nose, and relaxing breathing up his back, exhaling through an open mouth. His hands and arms move slowly through the familiar movements and he joins with nature, feeling one with everything that is arising, the dark sky, the cold wind, the lights from the city, the looming mountains, the opalescent ocean, and the far away islands.

As he relaxes he transitions into the "inner flute" breathing of Margo Annand's Sky Dancing Tantra. He breathes energy up from the earth through an imagined mouth in his perineum tensing his perineum in the same way he's pursing his lips. His eyes rise with his breath. He breathes out through a relaxed mouth, allowing his eyes to go down with his breath. With each breath he feels energy from the earth's fiery core rise through each chakra, energizing it, and then, finally, through his crown chakra as white light.

He slowly raises his hands in the large, slow opening movements of the Chinese yoga, Nui Gung (Inner Nourishment), and begins the practice of Circling Palms, moving in 360 degrees, channeling energy from the great sea of consciousness up through his heart to all of Santa Barbara, loving the life and consciousness there, and then outward, to all life and consciousness, and then outward to all unmanifest spirit.

Nature is compelling in cold wind, city lights, mountain shadows, and the Milky Way overhead, with a jet trail through it like a Chinese calligraphy character. Theo feels one with all nature, celebrating nature mysticism with psychedelic intensity. Consciousness glows up through the world, and Theo directs circling palms upward and downward in spirals, feeling one with the milky way, with the entire manifest universe, and with spirit beyond, before and after time.

The rows of house lights on the shoreline suddenly appear to be the line of light below lowered eyebrows in witness meditation. The sky is now Theo's consciousness, and he stands with his hands in his sleeves, relaxing deeper into the sea of consciousness we all share.

Just as he passes the boundary between his body and deeper witness awareness, a neighbor's dog (feeling a shift in the hilltop's energy) begins to bark. Theo is distracted back towards physical reality. He smiles, experiencing himself as someone falling off a high bridge into deep water, the deeper the better, and being magnetized back up to the bridge by the attachments of the world, the barking of a dog. Directing himself deeper, there is a moment of non-dual consciousness that flickers and subtly flows fuller. He surrenders to this, feel one with the void, sinks into the Shotokan kubadachi (horse stance), and is absorbed into deeper consciousness. Gradually, there is no time, only complete emptiness. The dog begins barking more insistently. Theo smiles and feels his consciousness slowly rise to the cold wind and panoramic view. The practice feels complete. *"I offer this practice to all beings, so that they may be free from suffering and achieve enlightenment."*

Climbing down the ladder and walking into his house, he hears laughter rising up the stairs. Sandy is watching the movie *Weird Science*. She smiles up at him, "How was your yoga?"

Theo smiles back, "Great."

Shifting perspectives to caring for wider circles of beings stretches development on central developmental lines. Balancing and channeling the energy of the earth and sky through your body is a blissful, healthy process. Improving and honoring intrapersonal and interpersonal relationships through healthy food, exercise, rest, integrations, attending to when you are opening or closing the moment, exploring and integrating shadow, healthy affiliations, and commitment to love and deep soul's purpose all support attuning body/mind/spirit with self/culture/nature.

Spiritual practice usually leads to peak experiences of deepest consciousness and blissful love. The more we direct our nervous systems into these states, the more stable these states become, until, if we practice long and effectively enough, they become traits. As we fuse with, and fill up, one worldview, we differentiate from it, and integrate into a new, wider embrace. Skip Alexander's research on TM meditation has generated persuasive scientific data that indicates spiritual practice accelerates growth on the self and other important developmental lines.[2] Such growth enhances movement through progressive worldviews towards experiences of unity with all.

One fascinating aspect of transcendent experiences is that we will interpret them from the worldview that is most natural and comfortable to us. Theo's worldview is mostly integral in that he has a felt appreciation for almost all points of view, and a diminishment of fear of death and loss. His spiritual practices draw from many traditions and include nature mysticism, deity mysticism, formless mysticism, and non-dual awareness. He feels his self as anchored in physical reality, as many energy bodies that include and transcend outward from his body and soul, and as different facets of the one jewel that is all manifest and unmanifest creation.

Michael at Hammonds reef.

Michael is surfing Hammonds reef with Don and Alex. It's 10:00 AM, high tide, and there is a five-foot late winter swell with wave faces sometimes almost twice as tall as Michael. The water is constantly in motion, and feels electric and cold outside their wetsuits. The unmistakable salt smell permeates the air. Only about ten guys are out since it's a weekday, and Hammonds is a second tier break (the first tier breaks like Rincon are always packed on a good swell). After a particularly good set in which Michael caught a thrilling right with his new six foot Channel Islands Swallow Tail (he almost got barreled by being enclosed in the circular open space of the breaking wave, the ultimate surfing experience), there is a lull, and everyone is sitting in the water, waiting for the next set, completely stoked.

A pod of dolphins are playing just outside the surf. Michael keeps watching them until he catches himself feeling like he is a dolphin, playing with his friends in the water. He looks around and feels completely one with the ocean, the dolphins, the coast, the mountains, his Dad and Alex. The sensation is intensely pleasurable. *"This is what Dad meant by nature mysticism last week."* He feels huge and wise, and like nature is an enormous feminine embrace holding not just him, but everyone and everything. Alex paddles over.

Alex: "It's so weird, Michael, you just looked like you got bigger."

Michael: Smiles. "I was watching the dolphins and I did this thing my family talked about last week." He looks over Alex's shoulder. "There's a set coming, I'll tell you about it later."

Michael is having a transcendent moment of nature mysticism, being one with nature, which deepens into deity mysticism when he feels nature as a huge Goddess presence. His worldview is partly mythological (he "mostly" believes in a sentient superbeing type God), and partly rational (he suspects science can explain almost everything) so he explains the experience to himself from both perspectives.

Humans tend to develop from a magic orientation (toddlers believe they can change the universe through their intent), to a mythic orientation (parents, or Gods, can affect our reality), to a rational orientation (everything can be explained by science), to a pluralistic orientation (everyone is equal and has equal access to spiritual experience, including oneness with everything), to a more integral orientation (all experiences have validity and fit together into hierarchies of optimal responses and understanding). Transcendent moments are interpreted by us from whatever orientation, or combination of orientations we currently inhabit.

Julie at N.A.

Julie has a more exclusively rational orientation than Michael, Nancy, or Don. The "higher power" of NA has been frustrating for her because, in her Goth tribe of the last two years, it has been an article of faith that religion is the opiate of the masses, that new age spirituality is hocus pocus woo woo, and that people kid themselves all the time about religion and God because they don't want to admit that we will all eventually die and be eaten by worms. On the other hand, she finds her NA meetings to be satisfying and intensely moving. She's at a women only speaker meeting later that night, listening to a twenty-two year old recovering heroin/cocaine addict named Sara. Though she's not consciously aware of it, she is engaging in a more descending, feminine practice than Michael. Where more masculine Michael feels spirit in big surf at the subjective edge of death (solitary because he is feeling alone with nature when he charges his wave), Julie finds spirit in community with other women, sharing pain and joy, loving and supporting each other:

> Sara: "And so I shot coke and junk, stole from my parents to feed my habit, and hung out with low-lives on Hollywood Boulevard. Finally I was selling sex to feed my habit and one night I cut myself on a fence running away from some cops. When they sewed me up at the hospital, they did a blood test and told me I was HIV positive." Julie is horrified by Sara's story. *"I'd rather die than have AIDS. How can she stand it, and how can she look so good?"* Sara continues. "Right there in the hospital I talked to God. I said, 'Please, help me,' and one of the nurses took me to an NA meeting. I've been sober and taking my meds ever since, and now I'm a junior in college. I want to be a counselor and help people like me." To her surprise, Julie finds that she is sobbing, tears running down her face. *"That's so cool. She's so beautiful now, and it was so ugly before. And she's HIV positive."* The women on either side of Julie put their arms around her, and she feels embraced by this community of women, all together to help themselves and each other. *"Remember this moment."* She tells herself. *"Remember right now when you want to use, or want to be mean to Mom or Michael."*

Since Julie has a rational worldview, she understands her experience as finding truth and goodness in a community of women, not as having a transcendent spiritual peak moment. If one of the other women tried to organize her story differently, for instance by saying "God is speaking to you right now," or, "You are relaxing into the one soul that we all share," she would find it irritating and presumptuous. The next day she describes the meeting to Mary:

> Mary: "What do you make of your experience?"

Julie: "I liked being one of those women. I admire Sara and what she's done. I'm so glad I didn't get AIDS or hepatitis, or get hurt like a lot of them. Sara was so cool, she wants to be a counselor and help people. I think I'd rather be a lawyer and work in the District Attorney's office. They can really help people like Sara get on the right path."

Mary: *"She would be such a good DA."* "Your parents will help you create that. Being a District Attorney is an important job. I love how caring Sara was. Research shows that, as women develop morally, they move from selfish, to care for their family and friends, to universal care for all, to universal care and universal rights[3]. It sounds like you had an experience of universal care for everyone."

Julie: "It felt so good. I like the meetings, but I wish they wouldn't talk about God so much."

Mary: "What irritates you about the God talk?"

Julie: "It's 'God helped me do this,'" or 'Thank God for that,' and nobody gives herself credit for doing the right thing just because she decided to."

Mary: *"Help her go deeper."* "How does it feel to you to give yourself credit for doing the right thing just because you decided to?"

Julie: "It feels good, but I also feel connected to all those women. During the meetings I love all of them."

Mary: "You all are probably having similar experiences, but are telling yourselves different stories about the experiences."

Julie: Not realizing her rational bias. "Why can't they see that it's them, not God, that has gotten them into the program?"

Mary: "What is it in you that decided to get into the program?"

Julie: "The part of me that wants to have a good life, and that loves my family."

> Mary: "Do you think you share those feelings with others, and especially those other women in the meeting?"
>
> Julie: "Yes, lots of people say they feel stuff like that."
>
> Mary: "Maybe for them, that shared feeling of loving others and deciding to do right is their experience of God."
>
> Julie: Getting it for a moment. "I see, we feel the same thing, but call it different names, or believe it comes from different places."
>
> Mary: "Who knows which perspective is the most right? One thing about death that I'm looking forward to is that I'll actually either disappear, or have answers to some of these questions."
>
> Julie: Confidently. "We just disappear after we die."
>
> Mary: "Either you're right, or you're in for a big surprise in sixty or seventy years." Both laugh.

Mary is exploring and stretching Julie's worldview by honoring her beliefs and exploring other perspectives with interest to look for commonalities and intersections. Like many good therapists, Mary cultivates the Integral felt appreciation for all points of view, and works to help Julie fully inhabit her current worldview, while simultaneously cultivating peak experiences and transcendent moments of wider embrace.

Don and Nancy in their sixty-fifth session.

It has been well over a year since Don and Nancy entered treatment, and much has changed. Even though their last session was three weeks ago, this meeting has, so far, involved them mostly relating good experiences they've had alone, with each other, and with the kids, and telling Theo how they successfully handled various problems:

> Nancy: Finishing a story where Don got home late and she was suspicious. "So I said, 'Why didn't you call?' and he said it was eleven and he didn't want to wake me."
>
> Don: "Not only was it the truth, but she believed me."

Nancy: "I trust you so much more now, so I told myself, 'Nancy, relax, calm yourself down, and call him. He's got a cell-phone.'"

Don: "But I was driving through that dead spot near Carpinteria and she couldn't get through, but she still didn't blow up when I got home. She heard me out and it was fine." His tone is respectful and admiring. He's proud of her for self-soothing.

Theo: "It sounds like you guys are doing so well we can go longer before our next appointment; maybe two or three months?" Nancy and Don look doubtfully at each other. Therapy has become almost a magical touchstone for them, but they also realize that their family system is currently open and healthy. Theo observes their looks and continues. "If something comes up and any of you want a session, just call. Otherwise we'll check in two months from now." They both nod. "Do you notice how different this is from our first session?" They all laugh.

Don: "I'm sorry I cheated on Nancy." Theo glances at her and she only barely recoils at this pronouncement. "But working on my marriage and getting the family involved was one of the best things we ever did. And Nancy was the one who insisted. I appreciate her so much for that." Nancy glows.

Nancy: "I love you so much more now. I wasn't really letting myself be a woman before. I like it." Don chimes in, "You like it, I love it." Laughter.

Theo: "The old defensive structures will always be there. You both will always have impulses under stress to go into the familiar defensive states, and sometimes you'll slip and start doing exactly what you did before. Development is include and transcend. One major difference is that both of you are now deep enough and wise enough to discern when defenses show up, and to know you have a choice to indulge them or reach for healthy responses. I can't tell you how much I admire the work you've done in service of health and love. Life is never perfect, but sometimes you wake up, and then never see things the same again. You guys have woken up in so many ways this last year. The cool thing is, there's always another level to wake up to if we keeping doing our best to grow and do right."

All therapy is about relationships moving toward unity.

The great paradox of all therapy being about relationships is that the more we attend to, heal, balance, and strengthen relationships with ourselves and others, the more oneness we feel with ourselves others, the world, and everything.

Relationships are dual by nature. One central way intrapersonal relationships are dual in that our observing ego is in relationship with our passing thoughts, memories, bodily sensations, and judgments, changing states, and shifting emotions—which also interrelate with each other. Interpersonal relationships are dual because they involve us relating to other people. The more we attend to and harmonize these relationships, the more integrated we become individually, and the more caring we become of others and the world, until eventually we can have progressively more moments of oneness with others, with nature, with all sentient beings, with all life, with everything that is arising in the present moment, and ultimately with the great fertile void from which everything has always been arising. Attending in healthy ways to the duality inherent in our existence leads us into progressively more moments of non-duality—of unity with all.

The psychotherapy session is a culture where a primary focus is supporting healthy awareness and integration of interior and interpersonal relationships. In each of the sessions we visited in this book, dedicated therapists and courageous clients cultivated compassion and depth of consciousness to support integration and growth, showing us the drama and magic of psychotherapy and human relating. I hope their experience—and the principles, information, and practices surrounding their experience—

has helped you become more aware of your own relationships with yourself and others and has supported your growth and integration.

Namaste`,
Keith Witt
June 14, 2008.

Endnotes

[1] Prabhavananda (1994)
[2] Alexander (1990)
[3] Gilligan (1993)

WORKS CITED

Adler, A. (1956). *The Individual Psychology of Alfred Adler.* H. L. Ansbacher and R. R. Ansbacher (Eds.). New York: Harper Torchbooks.

Ahrons, Constance R. (1994). *The Good Divorce: Keeping Your Family Together When Your your Marriage Comes Apart.* New York: HarperCollins Publishers.

Alexander, Charles N., and Langer, Ellen J. (1990). *Higher Stages of Human Development, Perspectives on Adult Growth.* New York: Oxford University Press.

American Psychiatric Association. *Diagnostic and Statistical Manual of Mental Disorders DSM1V.* (1994). Washington, DC: American Psychiatric Association.

Anderson, Walter Truett. (1983). *The Upstart Spring: Esalen and the American Awakening.* Reading, Mass: Addison-Wesley Publishing Company.

Assagioli, Roberto. (1965). *Psychosynthesis.* New York: The Viking Press.

Barbach, Lonnie. (1974). *For Yourself: The Fulfillment of Female Sexuality.* Penguin.

Baron-Cohen, Simon. (2003). *The Essential Difference: the truth about the male and female brain.* New York: Basic Books.

Beattie, Melody. (1987). *Codependent No More.* New York: Harper and Row.

Belliveau, Fred, and Richter, Lin. (1970). *Understanding Human Sexual Inadequacy.* New York: Bantam Books.

Berman, Jennifer, and Berman, Laura. (2001). *For Women Only: Overcoming Sexual Dysfunction and Reclaiming Your Sex Life.* New York: Henry Holt and Company, LLC.

Berne, Eric. (1961). *Transactional Analysis in Psychotherapy.* New York: Grove Press, Inc.

Bodansky, Steve, and Vera. (2002). *The Illustrated Guide to Extended Massive Orgasm.* Berkeley, CA: Hunter House Publishers.

Bradshaw, John. (1988). *Bradshaw on The Family: a Revolutionary Way of Self-Discovery.* Deerfield Beach, Florida: Health Communications, Inc.

Campbell, Joseph. (1949). *The Hero With a Thousand Faces.* Princeton: Princeton University Press.

Cloniger, Robert C. (2004). *Feeling Good, the Science of Well-Being.* Oxford University Press.

Curran, Dolores. (1983). *Traits of a Healthy Family.* New York: Ballantine Books.

Danielou, Alain. (1994). *The Complete Kama Sutra: The First Unabridged Modern Translation of the Classic Indian Text.* Rochester, Vermont: Park Street Press.

de Chardin, teilhard. (1959). *The Phenomenon of Man.* New York: Harper Perennial (1976).

Deida, David. (2005). *Blue Truth: A spiritual guide to life and death and love and sex.* Boulder, CO: Sounds True, Inc.

———. (2004). *Enlightened Sex.* Boulder, Colorado: Sounds True (audio recording)

———. (1995). *Intimate Communion.* Deerfield Beach: Health Communications, Inc.

———. (2002). *Dear Lover.* Austin: Plexus.

———. (2004). *Enlightened Sex Manual: sexual skills for the superior lover.* Boulder, CO: Sounds True, Inc.

———. (1997). *The Way of the Superior Man.* Austin: Plexus.

———. (2001). *Waiting To Love.* Austin: Plexus.

———. (2006). *David Deida, the complete recordings:* www.deida.info.

Dement, William C. and Vaughan, Christopher. (1999). *The Promise of Sleep.* New York: Dell Publishing.

Druck, Andrew. *Four Therapeutic Approaches to the Borderline Patient.* (1989). Northvale, New Jersey: Jason Aronson Inc.

Erikson, Erik. (1998). *The Life Cycle Completed.* New York: Norton.

Freud, Sigmund. (1949). *An Outline of Psycho-Analysis.* New York: W.W. Norton and Company, Inc.

———. (1952). *On Dreams.* New York: W.W. Norton and Company, Inc.

Gilligan, Carol. (1993). *In a Different Voice: Psychological Theory and Women's Development.* Cambridge, Mass.: Harvard University Press.

Gottman, John. (1999). *The Marriage Clinic: A Scientifically Based Marital Therapy.* New York: Norton Professional Books.

———. (2005). Presented at a conference, *The Anatomy of Intimacy.* Foundation for the Contemporary Family, UC Irvine, November 5 and 6.

Gray, John. (1992). *Men are from Mars, Women are from Venus.* New York: HarperCollins Publishers.

Haley, Jay. (1980). *Leaving Home: the therapy of disturbed young people.* New York: McGraw-Hill Book Company.

———. (1963). *Strategies of Psychotherapy.* New York: Grune and Stratton.

Hartmann, Thom. (2003). *The Edison Gene: ADHD and the Gift of the Hunter Child.* Rochester, Vermont: Park Street Press.

Harvard Mental Health Letter. *Meditation in Psychotherapy.* (2005). Harvard Medical School: Volume 21. Number 10, April.

Hedaya, Robert J. (2000). *How to Beat the Side Effects and Enhance the Benefits of Your Medication: The Anti-depressant Survival Program.* New York: Crown Publishers.

Hellinger, Bert. (2008). *The Phenomenological Approach in Psychotherapy Using Family Constellations as an Example.* www.hellinger.co.uk.

Johnson, Susan. (2005). Presented at a conference, *The Anatomy of Intimacy.* Foundation for the Contemporary Family, UC Irvine, November 5 and 6.

Jung, Carl G. (1961) *Memories, Dreams, and Reflections.* New York: Random House.

———. (1933) *Modern Man in Search of a Soul.* New York: Harcourt, Brace and World, Inc.

———. (1958) *Psyche and Symbol.* New York: Doubleday Anchor Books.

Kahneman, Daniel. (1999) *Well-Being: Foundations of Hedonic Psychology.* Portland, Oregon: Book News, Inc.

Kaplan, Helen Singer. (1974). *The New Sex Therapy: active treatment of sexual dysfunctions.* New York: Brunner/Mazel Publication.

Kegan, Robert. (1982). *The Evolving Self: Problem and Process in Human Development.* Cambridge, Mass: Harvard University Press.

Kernberg, Otto. (1975). *Borderline Conditions and Pathological Narcissism.* Northvale, New Jersey: Jason Aronson Inc.

Korzybski, Alfred. (1933). *Science and Sanity: An Introduction to Non-Aristotelian Systems and General Semantics.* Lakeville, Connecticut: The International Non-Aristotelian Library Publishing Company.

Lange, Arthur J. and Jakubowski, Patricia. (1976). *Responsible Assertive Behavior.* Champagne, Ill: Research Press.

Levine, Judith. *Harmful to Minors.* (2002). Minneapolis: University of Minnesota Press.

Levine, Peter. (1976). *Waking the Tiger: Healing Trauma.* Berkeley, CA: North Atlantic Books.

Liedloff, Jean. (1975). *The Continuum Concept.* Reading Mass: Addison-Wesley Publishing Company, Inc.

Linn, Denise. (2002). *Secrets and Mysteries.* Carlsbad, CA: Hay House.

Lowen, Alexander. (1975). *Bioenergetics.* New York: Coward, McCann and Geoghegan, Inc.

———. (1967). *The Betrayal of the Body.* New York: Collier Books.

Madanes, Cloe. (1983). *Strategic Family Therapy.* San Francisco: Jossey-Bass Publishers.

Maslow, Abraham. (1962). *Toward a Psychology of Being.* Princeton, New Jersey: D. Van Nostrand Company, Inc.

Masterson, James F. (1981). *The Narcissistic and Borderline Disorders.* New York: Brunner/Mazel.

Masters, William H. and Johnson, Virginia E. (1970). *The Pleasure Bond: a new look at sexuality and commitment.* Boston: Little, Brown and Company.

Minuchin, Salvador. (1974). *Families and Family Therapy.* Cambridge Massachusetts: Harvard University Press.

Musashi, Miyamoto. (1974). *A Book of Five Rings.* New York: The Overlook Press.

Neil, A. S. (1969). *Summerhill.* New York: Harold Hart

Nichols, Michael P. (2007). *The Essentials of Family Therapy.* Boston: Pearson Education Inc.

Prabhavananda, Swami, and Isherwood, Christopher. (1944). *The Song of God: Bhagavad-Gita.* New York: The New American Library.

Perls, Frederick. (1969). *In and Out of the Garbage Pail.* New York: Bantam Books, Inc.

———. (1992). *Gestalt Therapy Verbatim.* Gestalt Journal.

Phillips, Robert, D. (1975). *Structural Symbiotic Systems: Correlations With Ego-States, Behavior, and Physiology.* Chapel Hill, North Carolina: Robert Phillips, 100 Eastowne Drive, Chapel Hill.

Preston, John, and Johnson, James. (1990). *Clinical Psychopharmacology made ridiculously simple.* Miami, FL: MedMaster, Inc.

Ripley, Amanda. (2005). *Who Says a Woman Can't be Einstein?* New York: Time Magazine, March 7.

Roethke, Theodore. (1975). *The Collected Poems of Theodore Roethke.* New York: Anchor Books.

Rogers, Carl R. (1961). *On Becoming a Person.* Boston: Houghton Mifflin.

Sarno, John E. (1999). *The Mindbody Prescription: Healing the Body, Healing the Pain.* New York: Warner Books.

Satir, Virginia. (1988) *The New Peoplemaking.* Science and Behavior Books, Inc.

Schnarch, David. (1997). *Passionate Marriage.* New York: Henry Holt and Company.

——— (2002). *Resurrecting Sex.* New York: Harper Collins.

Schore, Allan. (2003*). Affect Regulation and the Repair of the Self.* New York: W.W. Norton and Company.

Seligman, M.E.P. (2002). *Authentic Happiness: Using the New Positive Psychology to Realize Your Potential for Lasting Fulfillment.* New York: Free Press/Simon and Shuster.

Shippen, Eugene, and Fryer, William. (1998). *The Testosterone Syndrome: The Critical Factor for Energy, Health, and Sexuality—Reversing the Male Menopause.* New York: M. Evans and Company, Inc.

Siegel, Daniel J. (2007). *The Mindful Brain, Reflection and Attunement in the Cultivation of Well-being.* New York: W.W. Norton

——— (1999). *The Developing Mind.* New York: The Guilford Press.

——— (2005). *The Mindsight Lectures: cultivating insight and empathy in our internal and interpersonal lives.* Mind Your Brain, Inc.

Siegel, Daniel J. and Hartzell, Mary. (2003). *Parenting from the Inside Out.* New York: Penguin.

Simonton, O. Carl. (1978). *Getting Well Again.* New York: St. Martin's Press.

Swimme, B., and T. Berry. (1992). *The Universe Story.* HarperSanFrancisco.

Tescher, Stacy A. (2005). *To Paddle or not to Paddle: it's still not clear in U.S. Schools.* Christian Science Monitor, March 17.

Thomashauer, Regena. (2002). *Mama Gena's School of Womanly Arts.* New York: Simon & Schuster.

———. (2003). *Mama Gena's Owner's and Operator's Guide to Men.* New York: Simon & Schuster.

Tzu, Lao. (1963). *Tao Te Ching.* Middlesex, England: Penguin Books Ltd.

Wilber, Ken. (2000). *A Brief History of Everything.* Boston: Shambhala.

———. (2001). *A Theory of Everything.* Boston: Shambhala.

———. (2000). *Integral Psychology.* Boston: Shambhala.

———. (2003). *Kosmic Consciousness.* Boulder: Sounds True (audio recording).

———. (2000). *Sex, Ecology, Spirituality.* Boston and London: Shambhala.

———. (2006). *Integral Spirituality.* Shambhala.

Witt, Keith. (2007). *The Attuned Family, How to be a Great Parent to Your Kids and a Great Lover to Your Spouse.* Santa Barbara Graduate Institute Publishing

———. (2007). *The Gift of Shame, Why We Need Shame and How to Use it to Love and Grow.* Santa Barbara Graduate Institute Publishing.

———. (1982). *An Investigation of the Effectiveness of Treatment Involving Talking Plus Touching in Enhancing Health.* Santa Barbara, CA: The Fielding Institute.

———. (2008). *Waking Up: Psychotherapy as Art, Spirituality, and Science.* Santa Barbara Graduate Institute Publishing.

Wolf, Anthony. (1991). *Get Out of My Life, but first could you drive me and Cheryl to the mall?* New York: The Noonday Press.

Wolfe, Tom. (1979). *The Right Stuff.* New York: Farrar, Straus and Giroux.

Wyckoff, James. (1975). *Franz Anton Mesmer: Between God and Devil.* Englewood Cliffs, New Jersey: Prentice-Hall, Inc.

www.ingramcontent.com/pod-product-compliance
Lightning Source LLC
Chambersburg PA
CBHW030309290526
45785CB00001B/277